Keeping Reptiles & Amphibians

TS-182

A Western Fence Lizard, Sceloporus occidentalis. *Photo by K. Lucas, Steinhart Aquarium.*

Opposite:
Lampropeltis
getulus
getulus, *the
northeastern
Common
Kingsnake.
Photo by J.
Iverson.*

Distributed in the UNITED STATES to the Pet Trade by T.F.H. Publications, Inc., One T.F.H. Plaza, Neptune City, NJ 07753; distributed in the UNITED STATES to the Bookstore and Library Trade by National Book Network, Inc. 4720 Boston Way, Lanham MD 20706; in CANADA to the Pet Trade by H & L Pet Supplies Inc., 27 Kingston Crescent, Kitchener, Ontario N2B 2T6; Rolf C. Hagen Ltd., 3225 Sartelon Street, Montreal 382 Quebec; in CANADA to the Book Trade by Macmillan of Canada (A Division of Canada Publishing Corporation), 164 Commander Boulevard, Agincourt, Ontario M1S 3C7; in ENGLAND by T.F.H. Publications, PO Box 15, Waterlooville PO7 6BQ; in AUSTRALIA AND THE SOUTH PACIFIC by T.F.H. (Australia), Pty. Ltd., Box 149, Brookvale 2100 N.S.W., Australia; in NEW ZEALAND by Brooklands Aquarium Ltd., 5 McGiven Drive, New Plymouth, RD1 New Zealand; in the PHILIPPINES by Bio-Research, 5 Lippay Street, San Lorenzo Village, Makati, Rizal; in SOUTH AFRICA by Multipet Pty. Ltd., P.O. Box 35347, Northway, 4065, South Africa. Published by T.F.H. Publications, Inc. Manufactured in the United States of America by T.F.H. Publications, Inc.

KEEPING REPTILES & AMPHIBIANS

JOHANN KROTTLINGER

CONTENTS

*Opposite:
Juvenile
Rough-scaled
Sand Boa,
Eryx conicus.
Photo by P. J.
Stafford.*

Behavioral Biology

Amphibians and reptiles, like all animals, have their own niches, their characteristic worlds. Between the animal and the components of its environment that are of importance to it exist virtually inviolate relationships. With its sensory organs it takes in various stimuli from its environment and reacts to them in a prescribed way. These lower vertebrates do not have the capacity to understand, to deliberate, to think, to comment in the human sense. Their central nervous system does not have the capacity to allow this. Nevertheless, the degree of recognition of the environment is defined by means of the capacity of the central nervous system with its often highly specific receptors, the sensory organs. Depending on the capacity of a particular animal of a particular species, the way it perceives its environment will be more simple or more complex in structure. The lack of a high-capacity cerebrum is to a certain degree replaced by or, more precisely, made up for by innate, species-typical instinctive reactions or hereditary coordinates, as Konrad Lorenz calls these fundamental units of behavior. They ensure even these lower vertebrates the opportunity to exist, to survive, to pass on their genes, in that each individual is and remains linked together with its own world. For these hereditary coordinates are just as inheritable as are form, structure, coloration, and markings, and are one of the characteristics of an animal species.

But individually acquired "information" can also make possible adjustment—acclimation to new situations that do not exist in the wild, as, for example, in captivity. These primitive vertebrates therefore also have the capacity to adjust to these new situations because of their ability to learn, the degree of which varies from species to species. It is possible to keep such animals under adequate conditions for a fairly long time in captivity only because they are capable of adjusting to even these often completely different

situations. In all stereotypes of hereditary coordinates, in opposition to these innate behavior patterns, behavior as a whole can be modified by "additional learning," but only to a certain degree. It is never a question of learning in a human sense with the associated understanding. The reactions of the animals to different stimuli only *seem* to be due to conscious thought; in fact, they cannot be, because the sequence of actions set in motion by a particular stimulus is fundamentally predetermined and not plastic. If, for example, only one link is missing from the "instinct chain," from the sequence of actions, and if a new situation that Nature has made no provision for arises, then the animal may react in a completely inappropriate way, such as by substituting an unrelated sequence of actions that would normally be used in a different situation. This complete breakdown in behavior suggests that most of the animal's reactions are not conscious but instinctive. Furthermore, these faulty responses could have disastrous consequences, disastrous not only for the animal, but also under certain circumstances for the keeper (for example, bite wounds).

Thus, under natural conditions, a lower vertebrate of this kind is properly adapted to its living space, in which everything is optimally regulated "by Nature." In this manner, even different animal species can live without conflict in the same territory without altering their behavior to an appreciable degree.

Different behavior patterns are governed by the type of stimulus that will trigger them, with which the particular animal will be confronted at a given time and with which it must come to terms. But not only do external stimuli play a part in this, so do internal stimuli, the internal state, in which the metabolic condition also participates (for example, hunger, mating drive). Studies have differentiated various functional spheres, of which one predominates and in general simultaneously excludes the others at any given time. Particularly important and conspicuous through their behavior patterns are the feeding sphere, the territorial sphere, and the reproductive sphere. Within a functional sphere everything runs, in a manner of speaking, according to a program, as long as no disruptive factor appears. The actions run along prescribed paths; within the reproductive sphere and the territorial sphere a specific "rite" or "ritual" has a clear meaning. Through this compulsory behavior, excessive actions are prevented or slowed down, in consideration of the survival of the species, of life.

At mating time, a specific territory is usually vigorously defended. But territorial species also persistently defend their domains against intruders,

A red color phase of the Eurasian Fire Salamander, Salamandra salamandra. Photo by J. Coborn.

A Red-eyed Treefrog, Agalychnis callidryas, *one of the more colorful terrarium inhabitants. Photo by B. Kahl.*

both of the same and different species, outside the mating season. Mates, mating rivals, and predators in each case trigger specific reactions. Certain reptiles, in particular, are extremely aggressive, both during and outside the breeding season. But this aggression is kept in check under natural conditions. "Intimidation behavior" and "threat gestures" precede the "fight," which is carried out according to prescribed ritual. Blows and bites almost never have fatal results, however, and are, in fact, often only symbolic. Furthermore, the winner is not always the stronger, physically superior individual, but often the acclimated resident of the territory, who thus enjoys a kind of "home field advantage."

The fight ends as soon as the defeated individual shows that it is giving up by assuming a "submissive posture." Subsequently, it is allowed to leave the victor's territory undisturbed. In some lizards, for example *Lacerta agilis,* the "loser" shows that it is conceding the fight by lying flat and "treading" with its feet before retreating. The goal of such a "fight" is thus not the death of the opponent; the innate, instinctive behavior maintains the life of both the individual and the species through "unconscious fairness." These innate "rules of life" virtually guarantee the survival of the species for the animal living under natural conditions.

Every animal keeper should at the very least concern himself with the fundamentals of ethology, comparative behavioral biology, in order to avoid making serious fundamental errors in the care of his animals, and also to get ideas for observations from an equally important and interesting aspect.

The Sand Lizard, Lacerta agilis. *Photo by H. Bielfeld.*

Basic Care

CAGES

Surprisingly, the living space of most animals is relatively small. They generally move on a few customary pathways in a limited area. But, even so, the living space in the terrarium is even more restricted. Furthermore, the living spaces of different species of reptiles and amphibians often vary greatly in size. It is thus logical to concern yourself first with the natural requirements for life, the movements, and the behavior patterns of the animals that are to be kept in the cages.

An animal makes a series of demands on the cage that absolutely must be considered. In the first place, sufficient space must be provided. It should correspond to the size of the animal; that is, the size that it will soon attain under proper care. Furthermore, the habits of the specific animal must be considered, above all the manner of movement and the sorts of places where the movement will occur (flat, open areas; branches; trunks; rocks; masonry; and so forth). Animals with "flexible movements," such as snakes and certain lizards, get by with relatively smaller cages than do animals with "ponderous movements" (tortoises, for example). There are some large terrarium animals that require relatively little space because of their principally motionless habits. Even these should, however, be provided with a larger run outdoors or on a balcony from time to time.

There are also relatively small reptiles that, as nimble runners or equally fast and agile climbers, prefer large surfaces in order to run wild in the truest sense of the word. Depending on the native biotope and the running or climbing habits, one selects longer or higher enclosures with appropriate furnishings. The plants also require a certain amount of space for optimal growth.

Even though we cannot simulate completely the climatic conditions of the natural living spaces in our cages, they should nevertheless be given as much consideration as possible. Adequate ventilation with the

Hyla gratiosa, the Barking Treefrog. Photo by W. B. Allen, Jr.

simultaneous maintenance of the necessary temperature through its entire range of variation must also be provided for, as difficult as this often is. Additionally, maintaining the proper relative humidity, which is also subject to variation in the area of occurrence of the particular animal, is difficult in a restricted space. Furthermore, the appropriate lighting conditions must be considered in the selection of the cage. Finally,

regular exposure to direct sunlight is a necessity of life for many terrarium animals, and one that you should not deny them.

The choice of building materials chiefly depends on the living space that you must imitate. The material must be resistant to variations in temperature and humidity. If you consider the two extremes of the desert and the tropical rain forest, the importance of this point will become obvious.

Wood is suitable chiefly

for terrariums that will be occupied by reptiles that like dry conditions. Hard, durable, aged oak satisfies these requirements particularly well. Because even a terrarium for desert inhabitants must be sprayed with water daily, the wood should be made more durable by means of a protective coat consisting of several layers of varnish. A terrarium of this kind with its natural wood grain also fits in well with the room furnishings. The bottom part of the terrarium holds the entire interior furnishings, including sand, gravel, fairly large rocks, and branches as well as the potted plants. It must therefore be strong and solidly built. Well-built joints (dovetails) prevent the individual sections from coming apart. Strong feet are attached to the bottom panel to help prevent it from rotting or

becoming moldy.

If you cover the bottom with a waterproof sheet of plastic (not less than 0.2 millimeters thick), several drainage holes in the bottom panel of the enclosure will prevent condensation from forming between the wood and the plastic. Rocks should not be placed directly on the plastic; instead, sheets of cork or styrofoam or a layer of peat should be laid on top of the plastic to prevent punctures. The wood frame that holds the side and cover panels must not be so heavy as to be obtrusive. The door in the front wall should be as large as possible to ensure easy access. More practical than a door is the installation of two panes that slide past each other.

A smoothly planed, solidly joined box can also be used as a makeshift terrarium. The corners should be strengthened

A terrarium for a desert-loving animal such as this South African agama, Agama aculeata, is easier to make and maintain than a terrarium or aqua-terrarium for water-lovers. Photo by G. Dingerkus.

with wooden braces. The box should not be too high and must have a cover of wire mesh, because the ventilation provided by a box terrarium of this kind is not very good. For certain bottom-dwellers such as toads and Slowworms, a cage of this kind is, however, quite suitable. A dry area can be created by using the same waterproof plastic. The cover of such an enclosure must be tight-fitting to prevent escapes. Ceramic boxes have the advantage of slightly cooling the interior of the enclosure even in hot weather if you keep them damp on the

Modern fiberglass tanks are efficient but not very attractive. They often are used by large-scale breeders and in laboratory situations. Photo by W. B. Allen, Jr.

adequate. To improve ventilation the box should be placed on a balcony so that it is exposed to some morning and evening sun. If the inside of the box is provided with a waterproof plastic sheet, you can prevent the buildup of moisture by punching a few holes in it. For salamanders and newts, which require an area of standing water, long, rectangular flowerboxes of ceramic and plastic are

outside. The porous material produces evaporative cooling. Of course, you can only see the animals in such a box from above, but since they do not like too intense light anyway, the enclosure will meet their needs.

Shallow metal-framed aquaria heat up easier in the summer. If the joints have become so leaky that water runs out, you can spray them regularly with cool water without having the water build up. Of course, this is only possible outdoors or on the balcony, where such aquaria belong anyway because of the improved air circulation. An air-permeable covering, such as nylon netting, is suitable for aquaria of this kind. A lead strip is sewn into the overhanging seam of the netting to hold it down. For animals that vigorously force their way through cracks and chinks, a cover of fine wire mesh with a solid frame must of course be used.

More durable than wooden cages are terraria of metal. Their chief advantage lies in their resistance to dampness and heat. It is essential to apply a protective coating of a non-toxic enamel in the desired color to the metal parts. Before building a terrarium of this kind you should first seek expert advice, since a detailed discussion of this subject is beyond the scope of this book. Every year new paints are introduced that are better suited for these specialized applications. Even plastic in liquid form can be applied.

For the frame of the terrarium use angle irons; the bottom is made of galvanized sheet metal.

The traditional first terrarium long has been a simple aquarium with an adequate substrate and cover. This still works for single specimens of many types of animals. Photo J. Dommers.

The strength of the frame and the sheet metal is dependent on the size and weight of the terrarium. A tightly inserted piece of sheet metal placed at an angle is used to separate the land and water sections. The separation between land and water must be watertight. Each should have its own drain hole.

The terrarium of the future will be made of plastic, which above all is not affected by moisture. The fact that our terraria must be reconditioned after a few years is principally due to the effects of water. When spraying an enclosure, you must always be careful to prevent the joints from leaking. Even so, the aquarium will eventually leak, when we will be forced to clear out the entire enclosure, clean it thoroughly, and, after the most painstaking removal of rust, cover the metal parts with a new protective coat. All of this would be unnecessary with a plastic terrarium. For animals and plants of the tropical rain forest, in particular, the regular spraying of the terrarium is of the utmost importance. Large terraria must be of constant thickness throughout to avoid weak spots. Whether plastic can fulfill this requirement in the long run remains to be seen, but you should try to keep abreast of technical advances in this area. It is to be hoped that one day we will have a material for building our terraria that meets all of our requirements: it should not be affected by heat and moisture over time, it must be easy to work with, and it must not be too expensive. Small, practical terraria of plastic have been built and have proved their worth. Distortion and warping have not appeared even at elevated temperatures (the upper limit is supposed to be over 70°C, 158°F).

The bottom section is constructed of glass panes, and silicone rubber serves as an adhesive as

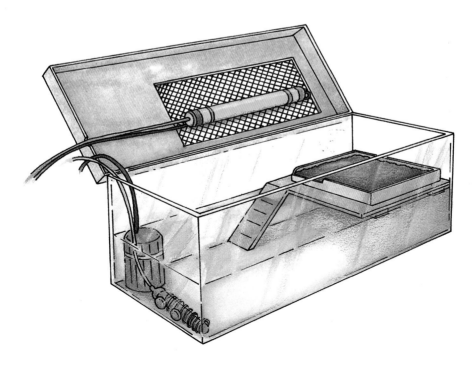

in all-glass aquaria. On this completely watertight bottom is erected the frame for the top part. The frame consists of glued together plastic sectional pieces with different cross sections that correspond to their function: angle cross, interior corner and exterior corner sections. Glass panes of two- to four-millimeter thickness (fitted to the size of the groove) are inserted in the side walls. The panes can be replaced in part by plastic mesh for improved ventilation. The frame for the cover is made of exterior corner pieces.

All of these sectional pieces can be obtained in hobby shops. A small terrarium of this kind is strengthened by the glass panes, so that one can certainly risk exterior dimensions of 50 by 30 by 30 centimeters, probably even larger. Depending on the use, a plastic bowl serves as the land or water section, as well as a container for plants. The fact that the panes can be removed and replaced at

Some animals just are not suited to an indoor terrarium or aqua-terrarium. This Spectacled Caiman, Caiman crocodilus, would never be at home in a normal cage. Photo by H. Bleher.

any time greatly increases the ease of handling of this "universal" terrarium. If the cover is built in three sections and provided with a handle for the middle section, you can easily reach into the terrarium from above without much danger that the animals will escape. This enclosure is also very well suited to rearing food animals.

You cannot make generalizations concerning the proportions and dimensions for a terrarium, but the dimensions should be based on the particular requirements and the habits of the animals.

Most terraria are quite heavy and can be placed on only a very sturdy table. There are lizards that live mainly, so to speak, "on the vertical." They spend most of their lives on walls, cliffs, and tree trunks. For these animals a "wall terrarium"

that is hung on the wall in the manner of a showcase is suitable. It should be wide and above all high; the depth or thickness is not as important. The diagonal roof, which may be folded up, holds the lamps in such a way that their warming rays strike diagonally against the rear wall. The frame of the front wall fits into a groove on the bottom and is fastened on top with a bolt. A frame of this kind can be changed at any time, which is critical for ventilation and sunning. In cooler weather or indoors a glass pane can be inserted in the frame. If the cage is hung on the balcony, this glass frame is replaced by one covered with wire mesh. This must of course be done very quickly, because precisely those reptiles for which a "wall terrarium" of this kind is suited are incredibly fast runners and adept jumpers. In order to make it more difficult for the animals to escape when you are working in the cage, it is beneficial to install a door in the lower half of a side wall. Because this terrarium is supposed to be hung on a wall, the interior furnishings must not weigh too much. Suitable materials for the interior furnishings include wood, cork, pumice, and styrofoam.

It is unfortunately impossible to simulate precisely the conditions of a natural living space, with all of its factors and its natural variation, in the terrarium. The area of a terrarium is simply too small to produce natural climatic conditions. Even though provisions for heating and lighting have been improving steadily in recent years, animals in captivity very often still lack one essential factor: sufficient fresh air. By fresh air is meant outside air; room air is not adequate.

The buildup of extremely dangerous stale air in the terrarium can be prevented by the use of wire-mesh windows. A narrow, 10 to 20 centimeters wide ventilation strip of wire mesh is installed on the bottom of one side wall and on the top of the opposite wall. When necessary, these openings can be covered with strips of plastic. With animals that are not too sensitive to cold, when the outside temperatures are warm

enough, the enclosure should be placed on the balcony. The front glass frame is then replaced with one covered with wire mesh. This arrangement will also provide completely adequate ventilation. It is not advisable to also provide the cover with wire mesh because of the accumulation of dust.

Supplying air for tropical animals and those that must be kept moist is more difficult. In this situation, a brass pipe with a diameter of about 1 centimeter is inserted through the wooden frame of the window so that

This group of trees in the Cayman Islands was home to anoles, geckos, and numerous insects that fed them. Obviously you cannot recreate a natural habitat in the terrarium. Photo by G. Dingerkus.

about 5 centimeters extends to the outside. A plastic tube connects this small pipe with a second that is installed right next to or on top of the heater in the cage. A suction is created in the tube line that draws the fresh outside air into the enclosure where it is then warmed immediately by the heater. The stale air is drawn out of a ventilation

need artificial heating of their cages at least occasionally; some also require additional irradiation. The coal and gas ovens used in the past have now been replaced by electric heaters in various forms. Although electric heaters doubtless are a great improvement, they make you completely dependent on a supply of electricity, which

slot located above on a side wall. One can also draw in fresh air using an aeration pump for aquaria.

HEATING, IRRADIATION, AND LIGHTING

Most terrarium animals

occasionally can be an inconvenience.

Heating cables with lead sleeves can be placed in not too tight coils on or in the substrate. They can also be run through water and wound around

Like many other burrowing snakes, the Kenyan Sand Boa, Eryx colubrinus, needs warm sand as a substrate. Photo by P. J. Stafford.

branches. They should be wound as evenly as possible in coils and should not be bent repeatedly in the same place, particularly in opposite directions. They must be free of kinks. Because of the danger of moisture, the plugs are connected to the extension cord outside the cage. This connection should be disturbed as little as possible. If the cables must be disconnected, then this should be done only at the wall outlet. Heating cables are available in various lengths and thicknesses. For fairly small cages and lower amounts of heat,

lighter heating cables with plastic sleeves are recommended. Their heating power is not too great, but the animals cannot burn themselves on them, which is a considerable advantage. In order to prevent snakes from strangling in loose coils, fasten them to something. When used to heat the substrate for animals that burrow, the cable is fastened to a styrofoam sheet with loops of perlon thread. A cable of this type can also be fastened successfully with the aid of heat-resistant polyester adhesive tape. With very energetic burrowers, such as the

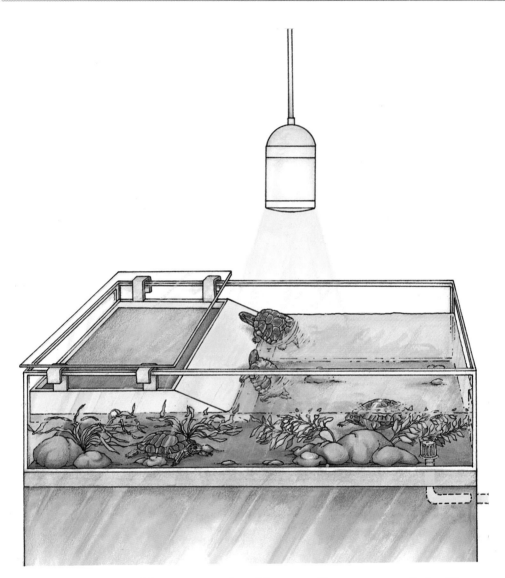

sand boas, you should check from time to time to make sure that the cable has not worked loose.

Although you can distribute a heating cable much the way you like in an enclosure, heat produced by a heating pad is localized and limited. Heating pads are available in various sizes and wattages; the larger ones may be equipped with a three-way switch. These heating elements are placed in the substrate and are covered with loose material such as sand or gravel, a wooden frame, a hollow gutter tile, or a stone slab.

Also useful are heating boxes of galvanized sheet metal, ceramics, and fired brick. The surface is given a natural appearance by using cement and gravel. If the rim is allowed to extend upward slightly so that a shallow basin results, you can evaporate water in it, which is of course very beneficial for many animals and plants. A narrow strip of brass mesh is installed in one side and another is added to the top of the other side. In this manner you produce a type of warm-air heating. Water should be prevented from entering the heating chamber.

Dry terraria can also be heated by means of a double bottom that is used as a heating space. Incandescent lamps in sockets under the false floor provide the heat. The false floor, which forms the floor of the terrarium, is perforated in one spot or provided with a wire-mesh window, so that the warm air flows upward into the cage. A hole in the side provides for the entry of fresh air. The heating space is accessible through a hatch because it must be cleaned and inspected from time to time.

The water section of a terrarium can be heated with a heating cable or a cylindrical aquarium heater. If this is

inserted in a hollow block it cannot be torn away or broken by the animals.

The specialist trade offers several types of lamps that are suitable for our purposes. The strength of the bulb and the distance the lamp is placed from the object to be irradiated must be tested. They are determined by the habits and provenance of the animals.

Plants may be placed only outside the circle of irradiation. If we screw a normal incandescent bulb into a reflecting shade we have both heat and light at the same time. If we place more emphasis on the production of heat, then a carbon-filament lamp is more suitable.

All radiation lamps are best placed above a wire mesh window in the roof of the cage so that there is no danger of burning the animals. In order to limit the amount of dust that

Except for some iguanas and a few turtles, reptiles and amphibians are seldom allowed to move freely far from their cage. Photo by D. R. Moenich.

Dart poison (or poison arrow) frogs such as this Dendrobates leucomelas require special terrarium conditions and care in order to thrive. Photo by K. Lucas, Steinhart Aquarium.

hung inside the cage, but you should make sure that the animals cannot get too close to them. A distance of 40 to 50 centimeters, depending on the strength of the emitter, must be maintained.

You should be even more careful in the use of ultraviolet emitters. They do good service in the winter months because only the combined presence of ultraviolet rays, vitamin D, and calcium ensures the growth of the majority of terrarium animals, above all the healthy development of bone. An average lamp should not be placed closer than 50 centimeters to the animals; a greater distance is even safer. Begin with an irradiation period of two minutes. With two to three irradiation periods a week you gradually reach a length of irradiation of ten minutes, which should not be exceeded. Even though reptiles exhibit an unusual tolerance for sun, one should still be careful with the dosage of artificial ultraviolet rays. Eye injuries have not yet been observed, but if at all possible prevent the rays from falling directly in the eyes.

enters the enclosure, the cover is divided into three parts. Only one section is equipped with wire mesh. The lamp is placed on this. At some distance under it, climbing branches are installed so that the animals can comfortably seek out the warming rays. When the lamp is turned off, cover the mesh window with a pane of glass or a sheet of foil.

Infrared emitters may only be turned on by the hour. Their rays penetrate more deeply and are only suitable for animals with an appropriately horny reptilian skin. The dark emitters produce practically no light and are used principally for crepuscular and nocturnal animals such as geckos. The light emitters produce a certain amount of visible light and are suitable for the irradiation of lizards, turtles, crocodiles, and snakes. These emitters are

Despite all technical advances, natural sunlight cannot be completely replaced. Do not miss any opportunity to expose all your terrarium animals daily to direct sunlight, which they require for their well-being. They also make this need known by their habits. The animals should have the opportunity to retreat into shade at any time while sunbathing. It should also be pointed out that panes of normal glass do not let ultraviolet rays through. There are, however, plastic sheets that are transparent to ultraviolet rays to some degree.

Animals that do not like or cannot tolerate harsh light should be exposed to natural rays only on cloudy days. However, even on overcast days with no sun, a certain amount of ultraviolet radiation is

Phelsuma cepediana and other Madagascar day geckos are the reptile equivalents of butterflies and hummingbirds, requiring a nectar diet, plenty of calcium, and lots of sunlight. Photo by K. T. Nemuras.

present.

In the light-poor time of year, supplementary artificial lighting is indispensable. Plants, in particular, grow in winter only when given sufficient supplementary light. Because the red component of light is essential for the growth of plants, you can simply use incandescent bulbs. The blue component is, however, of significance for producing a compact growth habit in plants. You can obtain a favorable spectral composition for most plants by using fluorescent lamps. The

long life, the high light output, and the modest amount of electricity used make them a truly affordable source of light. By means of special rheostats it is even possible to vary continuously the intensity of light.

Twelve hours of light a day is optimal for tropical plants and animals. With less intense lighting you can increase this time by two hours. Fluorescent tubes are best placed in a hood that is located on the roof of the cage. In this way damage caused by the humidity in the terrarium is prevented.

FURNISHING THE TERRARIUM

The choice of substrate is determined by the habits of the animals. Desert animals feel comfortable in desert sand. Because this is very difficult to obtain, we generally must make do with fine gravel and river sand, which should

be clean and as smooth as possible. To be avoided are dry peaty mold, dust-fine sand, and dust-fine soil. Snakes have been kept successfully on a substrate of coarse wood shavings. Shavings from pine wood, in particular, are supposed to be repellent to mites. Also suitable are large pieces of peat and peat bricks, which can be laid out on the bottom of the cage. If the peat bricks are laid dry and are then wetted, they will absorb the water and swell until the spaces between them have closed. One should exercise caution, however, when watering dried peat bricks in a cage that already contains animals. If the animals have hidden themselves in cracks and gaps, they will be crushed when the peat bricks swell as they absorb large amounts of water. One should therefore never allow peat brickwork of this kind to dry out completely. Loose forest loam is suitable for animals that like to burrow in the substrate. One should always sift it, however, so that dust-fine particles and pests are not introduced into the terrarium. Forest loam is also suitable as a substrate for arboreal terrarium animals. It absorbs moisture very well and thus maintains a high humidity level in the cage.

Many climbing animals

Every reptile and amphibian needs a secure, dark area in which to retreat from the strange world outside its cage. This Crotalus adamanteus under a bark hide was photographed by W. B. Allen, Jr.

like branches of various thicknesses. The perch is where they will stay most of the time. Suitable for this purpose are knobby, cracked branches of fruit trees with a relatively large number of branches in a small area. If the climbing perch will be free-standing in the cage, it is fastened to a hollow concrete brick or screwed into a wood base. This base is

*Most lizards
are climbers,
even species
such as
Eumeces
schneideri that
come from
deserts. Photo
by J. Wines.*

additionally weighted down with stones. Leaning the climbing perch diagonally against the back or side walls will provide a more natural appearance. Its branches are sawed off straight so that they will be solidly supported by two walls and a corner. Even if we do not use window glass in a terrarium but instead use reinforced glass, thick branches still should never be laid against the panes, but instead should only touch the frame. Make sure that, when spraying, the water runs down the trunk. It should not reach the joints of the cage and should not accumulate on the frame. The base of the perch thus should stand on the substrate. Attached patches of moss absorb the running water. Some animals like to lie over water. In such cases some branches of the climbing perch should extend over the water section.

For animals that prefer to stay on trees or in the branches, install not just one perch but two or more. The same applies to denser branches and shrubbery. These animals live exclusively above ground and are not content to constantly stay on one and the same branch. Even a

chameleon, despite its relatively motionless habits, moves and changes its location. Most arboreal snakes glide over and through the branches, which should be taken into consideration when installing them. For reptiles with

more or less specialized grasping feet, choosing branches of the appropriate thickness is critical. For amphibians, and reptiles that jump from time to time, you should install branches such as are used in bird cages, so that they have enough space to carry out aimed jumps. The expert can often tell from the body structure alone which "terrarium furnishings" a particular animal needs.

Animals that like to climb on wood and rocks need a rear rock wall. It is best to design the cage so that the back wall can be removed and replaced. Permanently covered rear walls can be effortlessly removed and cleaned in

this manner.

A true rock wall can be built only in large and correspondingly sturdy cages. Suitable as building materials are limestone slabs, the fragments of which are layered on top of one another in a diagonal course and are then cemented together. Gaps are reserved as hiding places or are filled with rich soil for the plants. A rear wall of pumice is constructed for the hanging wall terrarium. Two layers of pumice are installed one upon the other by gluing them or screwing them in. The cracks between the individual stones should be large enough that slender lizards can slip through them.

For tree-loving lizards and frogs, pieces of pine or cork oak bark are nailed to the wooden rear wall. Hiding places are

Toads, here represented by the attractive Bufo viridis, need cool, moist hiding places for their daytime sleep. Photo by J. Coborn.

produced automatically in the construction of such a bark wall. Fairly large hiding places are formed by attaching individual pieces of bark at an angle so that they stand out from the lower part of the wall. The animals are then protected from water that trickles down. In the wild they seek out such shelters when it rains. Many treefrogs like to perch on smooth wood. The rear wall for such a treefrog cage is constructed of palisade-like split beech trunks attached close together side by side.

Wood-covered rear walls should be replaced occasionally, because with time they could be attacked by mildew or could start to rot. Pieces of bark and cork, including sheets of decorative cork, as well as rear walls of styrofoam, are least susceptible to mildew attack.

Hiding places are easy to build on the floor of the cage. Any slightly curved piece of bark is suitable for this purpose. Rootstocks also provide good refuges and simultaneously provide places to sun in fairly large terraria. In mountain streams and on the seashore you may occasionally find rounded-off or multibranched, smoothly polished pieces of driftwood. When dried they are very light and are then particularly suited for

the wall terrarium. During the day, lizards like to rest on them when they are warmed by the sun. At night they hide under the often concave branches. Flat stones must be supported by smaller rocks. Also suitable are both ridge tiles and edging tiles, clay pipes, slotted bricks, crocus dishes, and orchid pots. These can be hung from the top of the cage or used in a planted, latticed orchid basket. Many terrarium animals favor such airy hiding places. Hanging or standing tree cavities (woodpecker boxes, chickadee boxes, and the like) can also be used as shelters. As far as possible, avoid installing the hiding places in the area of the rear wall of the terrarium. Instead place them in the middle zone, and the animals will generally become more "tame" and will adjust better to the "bustling" life in a human house.

To build the land section for fairly small aqua-terraria, look for old bricks with bottoms still intact but edges that are broken and rounded off on top. You can also smooth them off with an old coarse file in such a way that they serve as easy-to-climb riparian rocks. Hollow bricks can be planted to form overgrown islands.

Amphibians and reptiles that regularly spend a considerable amount of time in the water are best housed in an aqua-terrarium or a terrarium with an extensive area of water. This should always have a good drain. A root not only interrupts the water surface, but also give the animals the opportunity to cling to it and to better camouflage themselves.

The majority of aquatic terrarium animals live on soft, sandy, or "gravelly" substrates. For reasons of hygiene this substrate is often dispensed with because it quickly becomes soiled and filled with rotting matter. If you deprive animals that are accustomed to burrowing in the substrate to varying degrees of the opportunity to do so, then you take from them an essential

Plants suitable for the aquarium and aqua-terrarium are easily found in your local pet shop. The grass-like Acorus pusillus is an excellent bottom plant. Photo by E. Taylor.

element of life. Now that there are suction devices with which you can clean at least the top layer of the substrate without removing it from the tank, it is no longer necessary to dispense with a coarse sand or gravel layer of this kind. For a fairly coarse layer of gravel, a simple suction device is sufficient. Although the water flows out of the terrarium, the gravel is only raised into the lower enlarged portion of the glass tube and then sinks back into the enclosure after it is rinsed. For finer gravel a more complicated "bottom cleaner" is recommended. This is attached to an aeration tube. In this procedure the water and gravel remain in the terrarium. The strength of the suction stream can be adjusted to the diameter of the gravel. The decayed matter is collected in a bag. The animals can remain in the terrarium during a substrate cleaning of this kind.

Suitable as small water containers are clay bowls, which are available in various styles and shapes. Plastic containers are only conditionally usable. Their sides are smooth and they look unnatural. You can build your own small water containers in the desired form from cement

mixed with coarse gravel. Halved coconut and walnut shells, installed so that they are concealed, are not very conspicuous and are adequate for meeting the drinking requirements of the animals; for small frogs and toads they also provide sufficient bathing room. Bird water bowls are also quite useful. For reptiles that quench their thirst by lapping up dew or raindrops, install camouflaged drip tubes (mouse bottles) or small drinkers like those used for cage birds.

PLANTS FOR THE TERRARIUM

On the stage of the small, strictly limited world in the terrarium, the division of roles is somewhat different from that in the wild. Certain functions fade into the background or are dropped completely. This applies, for example, to plants as sources of food and as regulators and metabolic balancers. Plants still play an important role, however, as shelter and camouflaging cover in the terrarium. They also serve an important function as "backdrops" in the room terrarium.

A terrarium should, as far as possible, be a

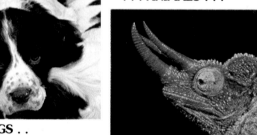

harmonious element in the interior furnishings of the room. Accordingly, both the animal and the keeper are forced to make concessions. At the same time, you should act on a large scale and not be too concerned with making everything look completely natural. The biological requirements necessary for the well-being of the animal must always be the most important consideration. It is also by no means absolutely necessary to use only plants. Were we always to try to hold strictly to the "slice of nature" and renounce concessions of any kind, we would soon run into difficulties. The number of plants offered on the market that are suitable for terrarium care is by no means as large as it appears at first. Many of the available and recommended terrarium plants grow—in an absolute and relative sense—too large. After critical selection only a few remain. Many plants that look so impressive in the greenhouse waste away from lack of light in the limited space of the often too humid and too warm terrarium. One should therefore ask experienced dealers or terrarium keepers for advice before purchasing plants and should also practice strict selection.

It has proved beneficial to replace many plants regularly and to keep them under better conditions, such as on a protected balcony, to recover. If you put the plants that will be used for the terrarium in pots, then you can replace them at any time without disrupting the entire furnishings of the cage. Besides the usual clay and plastic pots, "peat pots" are also suitable.

Many terrarium animals are not dependent on a thick planting, but instead need sufficient room to move or ample climbing provisions. In dry and hot terraria the plants in any case all too easily grow into the area illuminated by the lamp. In such cases it is quite sufficient to suggest or characterize the type of living space through one or only a very few plants. These should be robust in form so that they are not trampled.

Seek out native and garden plants and test them for their suitability. Quite persistent, for example, are polypodium ferns *(Polypodium)* and small-leaved ivy, which are available in various cultivated forms. Patches of moss are quite versatile but must be replaced regularly. Succulents, despite their occurrence in hot areas, need ample amounts of water. They can also decline rapidly if they lack fresh air, rotting in humid surroundings. Because of their lack of spines and their shallow root system, sanseverias are suitable; there are small, low-growing varieties in addition to the large, erect forms. More rewarding are the climbing plants, which need a certain amount of humidity. The wax plant *(Hoya carnosa)* has attractive, tough, smooth leaves. More delicate are the luxuriantly growing climbing figs *(Ficus pumila,* etc.).

In unheated aqua-terraria, small forms of calamus *(Acorus)* as well as snake tongues *(Ophiopogon)* thrive as long as you choose relatively robust varieties. *Tradescantia* species are indestructible. The uniformly green ones, in particular, are usable in both the unheated and heated humid terrarium. They grow in any substrate if they find sufficient moisture and can therefore be used to fill in gaps or empty spaces.

One biotope represents the pinnacle of the animal

and plant kingdoms in the terrarium: the tropical rainforest. For this biotope a profusion of plants is available to us that will indeed grow into a jungle if given warmth, humidity,

the necessary supply of fresh air, and above all peace and time to grow. With time this plant community will truly grow into an impenetrable tangle of incredible colors.

Despite its size, the fast-growing *Monstera deliciosa* is suitable for this tropical profusion. It needs only regular thinning from the base. The thick aerial roots reach to and enter the ground. With the aid of wide pieces of plastic tubing you can direct its growth in a particular direction so that you ultimately have a tangle of air roots. In size, the fairly small *Philodendron* and *Scindapsus* species harmonize better in the overall scene.

The center of interest in a tropical terrarium is, however, the bromeliads. These epiphytes grow on small branches and branch forks, which should be present in abundance. One can construct an "epiphyte branch" by boring artificial "branch holes" that have a drain hole on the underside. Epiphytes do not like to have their roots in standing water. A loose and permeable planting medium is stuffed firmly into the holes and depressions. After planting, the substrate is again pressed in firmly around the plant. The substrate consists of pieces of *Polypodium* root tangles or special epiphyte substrates that provide a loose growth medium. In

If you keep plant-eating reptiles such as this Red-legged Tortoise, Geochelone carbonaria, *it may not be worth your while to plant the terrarium. Photo by W. B. Allen, Jr.*

addition, shredded peat moss is added to absorb and hold the necessary moisture. Small pieces of twigs provide for further loosening of the substrate. Finally, mix in old shredded beech leaves. A portion of forest loam is beneficial as a supplement. The proportions of the individual components vary depending on the requirements of the particular epiphytes. A loose planting substrate is sufficient for species of *Tillandsia;* they also grow on the trunk itself if you tie them on with perlon thread or tempered copper wire. The ends of the wires must be bent completely into the trunk so that the animals do not injure themselves on them. The same applies to plastic-coated wire for flower arranging. Strips cut from old nylon stockings are well suited for tying on plants. The remaining bromeliads prefer a denser planting medium that must be replaced regularly because it rots and becomes porous with time. This planting medium is offered in prepared mixtures by garden centers that sell bromeliads and orchids.

Fairly large bromeliads as well as plant communities of smaller species grow quite well in orchid baskets hung in the terrarium with perlon thread. A thickly planted lattice basket of this kind is not only a very attractive sight, but frogs as well as other terrarium animals like to stay in it. With the aid of these baskets you can increase the ground space and produce a tiered terrarium.

Of the smaller types of epiphytes available on the market, the splendidly blooming *Tillandsia lindeniana,* the small *Tillandsia stricta,* and the relatively small *Vrisea psittacena* are suitable. As a ground cover the small *Cryptanthus* species are suitable, but they need a somewhat richer substrate mixture (for example, the addition of a third of peat and a third of evergreen forest loam).

The plants in a rainforest terrarium of this kind must be sprayed each morning with warmed calcium-free water. Most bromeliads live on the water that they collect in their leaf cups. They should be fertilized two to three times a week with a liquid or water-soluble fertilizer, which for bromeliads must be diluted even more than usual. Frogs like to sit in the leaf cups of bromeliads and contribute a quite sizable amount of their own fertilizer. When the water evaporates, residues remain that can be dangerous to the bromeliads in the long run. Therefore, don't just fertilize the plants, but also thoroughly rinse out the leaf cups regularly.

A ball sprayer is suitable for spraying from above, while a bottle sprayer is better suited for spraying from the side. They must supply water in the form of a very fine spray. (Should the sprayer ever fail to work, stuck ball bearings in the valve are usually to blame; they can be freed by striking the pump against a hard object. Sometimes the fine apertures of the nozzle become clogged; they can be cleaned with a razor blade after unscrewing the nozzle.) Also very well suited for spraying and misting are plastic universal sprayers.

You may become so enraptured by the beauty

and development of such a luxuriantly growing plant community that you finally turn the terrarium into a showcase for plants, giving preference to the plants over the animals. So as not to disrupt the balance of the beautiful exotic plant community, you

Elodea nuttallii is a soft aquatic plant this is easily purchased in pet shops and grows well in most aquariums. It is quite edible as well. Photo by L. Wischnath.

should only keep a few treefrogs in a tropical rainforest terrarium. Then you will experience, even in such a confined space, which is after all what a terrarium represents, the incomparable magic of the distant tropical world. Experiencing such a plant and animal community is

Toads such as this South African Red Toad, Bufo carens, prefer living insects as food and seldom do well on substitutes. Photo by K. Lucas, Steinhart Aquarium.

a highlight for many terrarium keepers.

FEEDING

Of the various functional spheres that make up and define the complex life of a wild animal, some lose a great deal of their significance in captivity or are sometimes even eliminated altogether. This means that the prey and feeding functional sphere moves even more to the forefront. In this area we can take action to prevent a weakening of the internal vigor of the animal. Many captive animals become conspicuously placid, almost lethargic. This is to be expected, for, after all, the animal has experienced a fundamental change in the hunting of the prey. Often it need not or even cannot hunt its own food any more. The human brings the food to it, even holds it out, and

the animal often needs only to open its mouth and snap it shut. These are radical changes that over time affect the physical condition and behavior of the animal in various ways. Not only is the internal vigor extinguished, but the animal's muscles also become weaker, and because of overfeeding the animal becomes more obese and more sedentary. Frogs, for example, remain at their favorite spots at the approach of the keeper and open their mouths even if he only holds out his finger. Although this may seem comical, it does have a detrimental effect on the animal itself in the long run.

Not only does the behavior toward the prey change fundamentally in captivity, but an unvaried and one-sided diet also results in demonstrable physical damage. The natural food supply of many animals varies substantially in the course of the year in both a quantitative and qualitative sense. At times a "seasonal food" is available in unimaginable quantities, and the animals literally stuff themselves until they simply do not want any more. Then they switch to some other food animal that the particular season offers.

Every keeper should draw up a food calendar for his region on which the time and area of occurrence of the various food animals are entered. Because of the continual advance of civilization, the situation changes from year to year, and it becomes more and more difficult to locate new sources of food. With the ability to procure freshly caught live food, however, stands and falls the possibility of keeping terrarium animals healthy and vigorous for any length of time.

The feeding of grasshoppers and butterflies appears to have special significance. These stimulate terrarium animals to energetic physical activity through their lively fluttering. It is interesting to see how a cage occupied by, for example, *Lacerta muralis,* anoles, or treefrogs suddenly comes to life when butterflies are introduced. You will no longer be able to recognize the animals! Even flies, a popular and natural food, do not produce such excitement. Through such experiences you will finally understand what it is that our terrarium animals chiefly lack. Furthermore, butterflies appear to be of great importance in a purely nutritional sense. Even weak-legged frogs that have become the victims of a one-sided diet for too long recover very well after temporary feeding with butterflies

If you can provide live insects such as beetles and moths, your lizards will enjoy chasing them as they would in nature. Lizards need exercise to thrive. Photo by E. Radford.

Snakes that need living food often are hard to keep and may present keepers with a moral problem—how do you reconcile feeding one pet (perhaps a frog) to another pet (such as a garter snake, Thamnophis sirtalis)? Photo by J. Dommers.

and moths.

These are only a few suggestions. A great deal more could and should be said about the manner of feeding. The limited space of this small volume, however, only permits a few spotlights to be thrown on this most important area of animal care.

A number of different methods of feeding can be proposed. Feeding with food forceps or a food stick simplifies the control of food intake. Above all, this method of feeding is useful with stunted, weak, or sick animals that refuse to feed on their own. Food forceps should not be pointed. Besides forceps of wood or plastic, those that bend to the side at an angle and have a club-like enlargement in front, such as are used by ear specialists, are suitable. A length of florist's wire or a very thin bamboo stick in which is stuck a pin (with the head of the pin protruding) can be used as a food stick. The impaled piece of food is moved back and forth in front of the animal until it is snapped up. Most terrarium animals learn this method of feeding very quickly and accept the food immediately. This method is chiefly used for offering substitute foods. Small pieces of meat are dabbed with one or two drops of a multivitamin preparation and are then fed. Lean hamburger mixed with a calcium-vitamin powder can be kneaded into small meatballs of lentil to pea size that are offered to the animals one by one with forceps or a stick. This supplemental feeding of calcium and vitamins is very important in wintertime. For fairly large animals that can swallow more sizable pieces, strips of the proper size are cut from beef heart. A pocket is cut into the meat with a scalpel, and the pocket is filled with a piece of a calcium-vitamin tablet or a suitable powder. It should be kept in mind, however, that these pieces of meat represent a very concentrated

diet and will swell up later. You should therefore cut the strips as thinly as possible and select a size that corresponds to the size of the mouth of the particular animal. This is especially important with amphibians.

The second method of feeding is the natural one: the terrarium animals must capture their own food. The food animals are simply placed in the terrarium by the keeper, and it is then left to the "hunters" to capture their prey. The keeper's task is to collect the food animals. To this end he must know where and when they can be found and how best to capture them. It is thus unavoidable for the keeper to learn about the habits of all suitable food animals.

Earthworms should not be collected in the vicinity of dung hills. They like to gather under doormats

Feeding living fishes to snakes and other reptiles and amphibians provides fewer difficulties both financially and morally. This Common Water Snake, Nerodia sipedon, is eating a shiner. Photo by R. Everhart.

and sacks that are kept damp. They are eaten most readily by terrarium animals in the fresh state when they still exhibit the "taste of the soil." You should feed them with the soil they contain and never clean out the contents of the gut beforehand.

You can also lure slugs in the same manner. Be cautious with snails collected in nurseries; it is possible that they could have been exposed to a snail poison. Garden snails are important for many terrarium animals because of their calcium content. Far too few terrarium keepers know

that numerous lizards readily feed on fairly small garden snails.

You can collect wolf spiders along the sides of paths or embankments with a plastic jar or with a plastic laundry sprayer, in which they can also be readily transported.

Grasshoppers are found in meadows and sunny, bare spaces with scattered vegetation. In some places they may be abundant, while in the immediate vicinity under apparently identical conditions not one specimen can be found. Place them in roomy cans loosely filled with grass and furnished with a wire-mesh cover on top and with an opening equipped with a stopper or a trap door on the side. Some types of locusts and bird grasshoppers can be reared.

Field crickets are lured out of their burrows with the aid of a blade of grass. Crickets are reared in abundance and sold on the market. Be careful when transporting them. Always cool them first!

Flies are becoming less and less common in the city, but in stables you can collect them even in wintertime. They are most easily baited with meat (fish, lung), cheese, and sugar to which a few drops of beer have been added. The bait must not be allowed to dry out too rapidly. A fly trap works because of the fact that the flies do not fly to the side when leaving the bait, but instead fly up into a kind of basket. An improvised fly trap is easily constructed from wire mesh. The wire mesh is bent in such a way that two funnels that fit one inside the other are formed, each with a hole in the end that is just large enough for a fly to get through. The top hole is closed with a stopper and is only opened to remove the flies. The bait is hung on a wire in the lower, shallow funnel. Because flies move toward light, it has proved practical to cover the lower part of the trap with a strip of dark paper, cloth, or sheet metal. Fly maggots are also a useful food as long as not too many of them are fed at one time. Blowflies like to lay their eggs on a small

Tiliqua scincoides, *a large, popular Australasian skink that will accept crickets as well salad and will even take dog food. Photo by J. Wines.*

This Leopard Gecko, Eublepharis macularius, *is making quick work of a large locust. Diversified feeding is necessary for almost all reptiles and amphibians. Photo by M. Gilroy.*

piece of rotting meat. The maggots grow on this very rapidly.

Mealworms are easy to keep and rear. The wide container (box, ceramic vessel) in which they are kept must not be allowed to become damp, and its cover should be permeable to air. The container is filled half full with wheat bran. Feed the mealworms (both adult and larvae) dog pellets, bread, vegetables, lettuce, and fruit (but nothing too wet). They can also receive grain grist (wheat, corn) and, for moisture, small pieces of carrot, fruit, and fresh bread. Folded cloth or corrugated paper serves

for the laying of the eggs. Mealworms are a one-sided food and are unsuitable for feeding over long periods of time. They are fine when there is a shortage of other foods.

"Meadow plankton" represents a nutritious fresh food for small lizards and frogs. A butterfly net or a wire-mesh funnel attached to a long stick is used to sweep through meadow plants. At home, store the "harvest" in the refrigerator until the insects and spiders are stunned by the cold. Then they can be sorted easily and placed in the terrarium.

Wax moths are an

excellent food, and it pays to rear them. Their caterpillars are also readily eaten. Butterflies are caught with a net or are baited. Moths are easily collected using ultraviolet light. Smooth caterpillars are also readily eaten. Collect food in places where no pesticide use is suspected.

Automatic feeding arrangements on the balcony or in the garden have various advantages. They are suitable primarily for fly-eating terrarium animals. A fly trap is installed on the underside of a wall terrarium in such a way that the flies, when they have reached the second funnel of the trap, crawl directly into the terrarium through the topmost opening.

Terrarium animals that are not able to crawl up smooth glass walls or the corners of the cage are kept in a roomy glass container that is as tall as possible and open on top. The container must, however, be protected against exposure to strong sunlight. On the bottom place a piece of fish, meat, or cheese that is used to attract flies. Soon the terrarium inhabitants gather around this source of food, which is automatically replenished again and again.

Cyrtodactylus pulchellus is an uncommon gecko that prefers live food insects. Photo by K. T. Nemuras.

Illnesses

Because for all practical purposes we still know virtually nothing about the illnesses of terrarium animals, this chapter is quite discouraging. We can expect successful recoveries with only a few illnesses at present, although research is being done on this sector of veterinary science.

It is important to be able to recognize a sick animal as such as soon as possible. Changes in its habits in comparison to those of a healthy animal usually quickly attract notice. Lack of movement, changed appearance of the skin, and refusal of food indicate that something is not right with the animal. If an animal lies in the cage conspicuously limp and in an abnormal posture; if it no longer seeks out or leaves its hiding place; if the mouth remains open for a long time; or if foamy, watery, or slimy bubbles are visible on the nostrils and in the mouth opening, then without doubt we are faced with a pathological disorder. Animals that become emaciated or swell up for no apparent reason are also ill.

Salamanders occasionally exhibit open, ulcerous areas of skin. Sometimes the limbs and the tail rot and fall off. As with all sick animals, isolate them immediately and give them fresh water as often as possible. Best of all is flowing water. If this does not bring success, an attempt with a weak solution of potassium permanganate is worthwhile. Under certain circumstances one must amputate the limbs with a quick snip of the scissors. In the event that these artificially produced wounds are attacked by fungus, treat them like bites, with fresh water and potassium permanganate.

Dropsy in salamanders has a number of causes. Besides freshwater treatment, nothing decisive can be done. Large accumulations of air in the bellies of newt and salamander larvae often go away on their own after a while. A special treatment besides fresh water is pointless because we do not know the causes of the illness.

Salamanders occasionally have difficulty in shedding their skins.

Unless your Fire Salamander, Salamandra salamandra, develops sores or ceases feeding, it will be hard to tell when it is sick. Recognizing a sick pet is over half the solution to the problem. Photo by K. Lucas, Steinhart Aquarium.

When kept in close quarters with minimal sanitation, frogs (such as this Mink Frog, Rana septentrionalis) may develop red-leg, a serious bacterial infection. Photo by R. T. Zappalorti.

Place them in a container very thickly planted with *Tradescantia* and carry out frequent water changes. There they perhaps will succeed in casting the skin among the tangle of plants and roots.

Frogs sometimes exhibit lameness of the visibly weak hind legs. This is often an indication of vitamin B deficiency. In other cases you can see a softening and deformation of the bones. Alter the diet to include vitamin B, vitamin D, and calcium. If convulsions occur, then you must consider the possibility of calcium deficiency or poisoning with insecticides. If a red coloration appears on the belly or the legs, especially in treefrogs, immediately place the animals in a thickly planted, well-aerated *Tradescantia* container that is placed outdoors and is sprayed as often as possible with fresh water. A prolapse of the gut can rarely be healed permanently, but you can carefully push it back with a moistened or oiled cotton swab.

Toads are sometimes attacked in the nasal and mouth cavities by parasitic flies and may be destroyed (literally eaten up) from the inside out. One accomplishes little by the removal of the visible larvae and disinfection. Destroy infected animals in order to avoid endangering the remaining stock.

Lizards are also subject to limb lameness, which should lead you to suspect symptoms of deficiency or poisoning by pesticides. A treatment with vitamin B sometimes, but unfortunately only rarely, is successful. We also cannot yet do much about the gradual withering away of the toes and the tip of the tail.

Softening and deformation of the shell in turtles are indications of vitamin D deficiency. We can successfully treat deficiency damage of this kind with doses of vitamin D, calcium, and ultraviolet rays or natural sunlight. Watery eyes, often associated with blindness or inflammation of the lids, are treated with eye ointment, doses of vitamin A, and warmth. In these cases it is often a question of a pathological change of a gland in the eye socket, the cause of which is still unknown and therefore cannot be corrected. Aquatic turtles, like the majority of reptiles and amphibians, are carriers of worms. Regular water changes at least prevent a cumulative self-infection in the unlikely event that the necessary change of hosts of the parasites is possible.

In crocodiles, in particular in very young specimens, vitamin and calcium deficiency symptoms often appear

Lizards fed an inadequate diet often suffer from rickets and other skeletal deformities. This Leopard Gecko obviously had a balanced diet as a baby. Photo by K. T. Nemuras.

and can be treated.

If snakes have difficulty in shedding their skin, administer a lukewarm bath for several hours. You must ensure that they receive sufficient air through the nostrils. Weak or chilled animals should not be subjected to such a procedure. By oiling with cod liver oil or any other oil, the skin can sometimes be softened and removed. This must be done very carefully, particularly in the head region and on the eyes. Treat pustules with dry heat. If ulcers have formed, use a healing ointment with sulfonamides, antibiotics, or even corticosteroids. In arboreal snakes a spraying treatment is practical because the animals do not feel disturbed and thus do not rub off the ointment immediately by crawling around. With the dreaded stomatitis, treatment with a local antibiotic (in an ulcerous infection with a corticosteroid) is appropriate. One should, however, be cautious with these medications and should first ask an expert about the dosage and the advisability of such a

A "Snow Corn," an albino mutant of the Corn Snake, Elaphe guttata. Photo by J. Wines.

treatment.

Against mite infestation, complete success is achieved by spraying the cage including the animals with Neguvon, which is employed in veterinary medicine, in a 0.2 percent solution. This treatment can be repeated after a week. Ticks are also sprayed with the same material in the event that dabbing with alcohol is ineffective. They must be detached carefully. The head must never be allowed to remain imbedded in the skin of the afflicted reptile.

If you are compelled to attempt forced feeding, then you should leave this to an expert. It may be carried out only with extreme caution and demands an exact knowledge of the mouth and swallowing organs. Concentrated liquid food is administered with a syringe to which a bicycle valve tube is attached; this is replaced by a curved hollow probe with animals that have a strong bite.

Ulcers, that is open skin defects, are bathed in camomile solution or, more effectively, in potassium permanganate or trypaflavin (10 milligrams per 1 liter of water for both). With fairly large, viscous, pus-covered sores of terrestrial amphibians and reptiles, try an ointment or a spray with sulfonamides, antibiotics, or synthetic adrenal cortex preparations. These medications must be obtained from a veterinarian. Antibiotics can be administered to these animals in high dosages (up to ten times the human dosage!). If ulcerous and tumorous growths are present, also consider the possibility of fungus diseases.

The cause and origin of growths and tumors must first be determined. If it is a question of pustulent abscesses, lancing followed by syringing with an antibiotic has proved effective. True tumors must be surgically removed.

Worm infestation of the alimentary canal must be treated by a veterinarian, if only because of the problem of determining the proper dosage. Thibenzol (150-200 milligrams pure substance per 1 kilogram of body weight) and Piperazin (100 milligrams per 1 kilogram of body weight) have proved effective. Both of these medications should be purchased through a veterinarian. They are administered with the food, either mixed in with it or injected into it (for example, into mice). If this is impossible or inadvisable for any reason, there is no choice but a direct injection performed by a doctor or veterinarian. The administering of high-grade antibiotics should be coupled with doses of vitamin B.

Baby turtles such as this Podocnemis expansa *from Brazil often are very difficult to raise because they require a rich, varied diet with plenty of calcium as well as excellent light conditions. Photo by H. Schultz.*

Selecting A Terrarium Animal

Before purchasing an animal you should have already confirmed that you are truly in the position to provide the conditions necessary for its well-being.

It often happens that beginners buy the animal and the cage at the same time, yet this should be avoided in the interests of the animal. Newly captured or imported animals that make a healthy impression belong in a completely and properly furnished cage that has been ready for several days at least. This also applies to a quarantine period, should it prove necessary.

The theoretical and practical preparations for the housing and care of the animals should be completed at your leisure. It is advisable, before the purchase of amphibians and reptiles, to learn as much as possible about their habitat as well as their habits. In other words, you should try to obtain as precise data as possible about the collecting site. Knowing the country of origin alone is not sufficient, because completely different climatic conditions often prevail in the northern and southern parts of even fairly small countries. If the dealer is unable to provide the exact information, which will usually be the case, particulars on the range of the animals can be found in specialist literature. In handbooks of geography you can also find additional information about the climatic and other conditions. Equipped with this knowledge you can then proceed with the furnishing of the terrarium with a good conscience.

A prerequisite, of course, is that the necessary space and other requirements for life are available for the animals that are to be kept. Of particular significance is feeding. Check ahead of time to see whether the necessary food can be purchased in sufficient quantity, quality, and variety throughout the year. Because of the abundant food supply

The bright eyes and tight skin of this Green Anole, Anolis carolinensis, are signs that it is a healthy animal. Photo by M. Gilroy.

available, the late spring is the best time for purchasing terrarium animals. At this time an ample assortment of fresh food animals and plants is available. Before the onset of winter you should set up your own food cultures.

crepuscular animals). If reptiles have suffered from thirst for a fairly long time in captivity, they often rush to the water container at the first opportunity and literally pump themselves full. This can be their undoing. At

Before you buy a pet, be sure to see it feeding or you may be asking for trouble. This Mole Salamander, Ambystoma talpoideum, was photographed by W. B. Allen, Jr.

When buying an animal, always ask with what and how often it was fed and when it was last fed. Some amphibians and reptiles from warm climates usually refuse to eat for a long time because they were kept at too cold a temperature or because they were not fed at the proper time (for example,

first give them only the opportunity to quench their thirst gradually in small portions. If the animal in question is dehydrated, initially give water containing 1% of sea salt before gradually switching to a 0.6% salt solution and finally to normal drinking water.

The author had a newly

purchased Leopard Snake drink itself to death hours after being placed in the terrarium without supervision. Only then was it discovered that the animal had received neither food nor water for weeks in a pet shop. Another example was shown by a mass importation of Russian Tortoises. Some of these animals were not only saved several of these turtles. Later they drank the juice from a halved tomato before subsequently also eating the soft flesh. When, several days later, they began eating lettuce with vitamin supplements, feeding them was no longer so difficult. You can attempt to give lizards water by means of an eyedropper or pipette. The

The Black Toad, Bufo exsul, is an endangered species. Anyone keeping such a protected species should be experienced in all aspects of its care. Photo by K. Lucas, Steinhart Aquarium.

emaciated but were also severely dehydrated. They were in a condition of high-grade dystrophy with dehydration. Because of the loss of water and salts, the water-salt ration and with it the remaining metabolic processes were thrown out of balance. A condition of this kind is extremely threatening and demands immediate and drastic intervention. An immediate treatment with a weak salt-water bath diet should include large amounts of protein to help the body rebuild. In this area there are still many things to learn and methods to work out.

After the purchase, there are difficulties in some cases because the particular animal is in poor condition or suffers from an illness. A situation of this kind is extremely disagreeable for both parties, the buyer and the seller. The question of how

Many young Boa Constrictors, Boa constrictor, die before reaching maturity due to intestinal worms and respiratory diseases. Keep them warm and see your veterinarian about a suitable wormer. Photo by B. Kahl.

the present condition of an animal and the further prospects of its well-being can be judged is therefore completely justified. Many disappointments can be avoided if you know the signs that indicate whether everything is in order with the animal or not. For this reason, there follows a brief discussion of what one must consider when a terrarium animal changes hands.

The animals must be vigorous and must express this through their body carriage. Depending on the species's temperament, they should exhibit a lively nature and their typical coloration at the customary temperature. After temporary exposure to cold or fairly long shipping, however, judging these traits is possible only after keeping them for some time under favorable conditions.

In particular, reptiles and amphibians in a healthy state take an interest in their environment and react to the new keeper, even if not in a positive sense at first. The fact that newly caught animals may exhibit certain warning and fear reactions must also be considered. Energetic attempts to avoid and escape from the keeper are characteristic of a healthy animal that is not yet acclimated. When placed on its back it must return itself to the normal position vigorously and quickly. A slow and weak reaction is not a good sign.

The body should be uniformly rounded and not gaunt. Conspicuous longitudinal folds are generally an indication of emaciation. Contours of pelvic bones, ribs, and vertebrae must not be clearly visible through the skin, and the eyes must not be sunken in their sockets, distended, or protruding. In salamanders and lizards, pay attention to the thickness of the base of the tail: fat is often stored here in a healthy animal.

The skin of a healthy terrarium animal is free of defects, without wounds or

Secretions from the mouth and nasal openings indicate colds; sometimes you can even hear distinct sniffling. If an animal breathes heavily for a long time with a wide-open mouth, then an illness of the respiratory organs should be suspected. The tongues of lizards and above all of snakes must dart out in a lively manner.

ulcers. Look for scraped snouts. Tumors, pustules, and ulcers are to be ruled out. Amphibians should not present a bloated appearance; frogs should not have extended, trembling legs or glassy, swollen red thighs; reptiles should have no ticks or mites; and turtle carapaces should not be soft.

The droppings must also be examined and should possibly be subjected to a microscopic examination. Worm infestations, for example, are not rare. Of the infectious intestinal illnesses, two in particular must be taken seriously: amoebic dysentery of terrarium animals, which is occasionally introduced, and abscesses of the liver

Tortoises such as this Testudo hermanni *need regular access to sunshine and must not be kept too moist. Always provide a varied diet. Photo by B. Kahl.*

Any reptile or amphibian can carry salmonella bacteria, so always wash your hands before and after handling your pet, even a captive-bred Leopard Gecko, Eublepharis macularius. Photo by K. T. Nemuras.

and large intestine, which can develop under certain conditions and cause the animal to waste away. It is reassuring that transmission to humans is supposed to be impossible. Unfortunately, humans are not immune to the *Salmonella* bacteria that infect this class of the animal kingdom. Disinfecting your hands after handling amphibians and reptiles is therefore always recommended, above all if you suspect that they are ill, which of course requires a veterinary diagnosis.

All animals that are obviously ill or are suspected of being ill or are in poor condition from unknown causes should be kept for a couple of weeks in a sterile quarantine terrarium, where they are kept under conditions of the strictest hygiene until you are sure of their condition.

Take plenty of time to make all critical observations and, as far as possible, finalize the purchase only when the health of the animal is guaranteed or a brief "test period" is granted.

ACCLIMATION

When good hiding places are available, a new animal will often stay concealed for a long time, sometimes too long. But if we deny it the opportunity to retreat into a hiding place, then it could possibly run itself to death in fright, particularly against the still unfamiliar transparent glass panes. In the acclimation of many terrarium animals, it has proved beneficial to install densely leaved branches in the cage. In this dense green foliage, whether climbing branches or ground cover, the animals feel relatively safe and observe the approaching keeper without trying to escape. Little by little the leaves dry and fall off, and with the gradual thinning of the foliage the shy inhabitants will soon develop confidence in the new situation. Finally, you can carefully remove this temporary camouflaging material without eliciting drastic defense or escape responses. The author has experienced this with frogs, lizards, and snakes.

The process of

acclimation is accelerated and made easier above all by feeding. If you initially let the new acquisition go without food and possibly without water and also raise the temperature of the cage (with animals that can tolerate it), then an acceleration of the metabolic processes will result and the feeling of hunger and the state of excitement will increase. At this point notice how, in many cases, escape behavior and feeding behavior will, in a manner of speaking, clash with each other, how both functional spheres overlap until one displaces the other. Finally, the animal takes food from the forceps or even from the hand; water drops are taken even from an eyedropper or the finger tips. Once extreme thirst

Many snakes adapt well to captivity, especially if they are given plenty of hiding places. Never neglect the fact that reptiles and amphibians need to hide most of the day. Photo of Natrix maura by B. Kahl.

Top: A two-tailed Five-lined Skink, Eumeces fasciatus.
Below: *Hyperolius marmoratus. Photos by K. Lucas, Steinhart Aquarium.*

and hunger have been satisfied, the particular animal will again cautiously withdraw, and escape behavior is often triggered once more.

Associating a newly acquired animal with established ones must be closely monitored. If violent fights occur in a closed terrarium, the instinctive protective behavior patterns will ultimately fail within the limited confines of the terrarium because the defeated animal will not be able to leave the territory, since the terrarium of course is smaller than the territory that would be present in nature. Under these conditions a fight may come to an unnatural conclusion precisely because of the unnatural space restrictions in captivity. The defeated animal often dies because Nature has not provided for these unnatural conditions.

For the same reasons, juveniles often are eaten by adults in the terrarium. These animals do not recognize a "sense of family," and they do not exhibit true social attachments. They usually only gather at communal sunning places or

favorable feeding sites as well as communal winter dens.

When purchasing animals it is not just a question of the animal becoming acclimated to new conditions. The keeper should also make the effort to understand, as far as possible, the individual world of his animals.

TRANSPORTING TERRARIUM ANIMALS

If you must have terrarium animals shipped, always make sure that the recipient is home and in the position to accept the shipment immediately. The fastest mail or air connection should be chosen without consideration of cost. For fairly small animals, a strong carton is sufficient; larger ones are shipped in sturdy crates. A few air holes are sufficient. Packages of this kind should always be markied "live animals." In addition, it also should be stressed that the shipment, depending on the season, must not be stored at too hot or too cold a temperature and absolutely must be protected against sun and frost. The best way to ship is by express after previous notification by telephone. Some shippers

Unless you can provide the proper cage conditions, such as a hot, dry, rocky terrarium for this sungazer, Cordylus giganteus, do not buy the animal. Photo by J. Coborn.

animals should never be transported wet.

If you pick up your own animals or take them along on a fairly long trip, you should avoid letting them get too cool at night in the motel room. Heating the shipping container by means of a heating cable or a heating pad has proved effective.

Aquatic animals such as this Xenopus laevis can be transported in ordinary plastic bags like those used for tropical fish. Photo by K. Lucas, Steinhart Aquarium.

will accept virtually all animals, while others may reject snakes. Check to make sure there are no problems.

No feeding is done before shipping. The shipping container is padded with moss or lightweight foam plastic. The animals are placed individually in linen sacks or perforated plastic bags. Tin cans can also be used; they have the advantage that they cannot be crushed as easily as sacks and plastic. Holes in the top of the can must be punched from the inside out, because otherwise the animals could be injured on or could rub against the jagged metal of the stamped holes, even if these have been beaten flat. Depending on their need for moisture, damp moss or slightly moistened small pieces of foam plastic are added with the animals. Terrarium

COLLECTING YOUR OWN SPECIMENS

The equipment that you can bring along on collecting trips is determined by the mode of transportation—a car holds more than a backpack. A terrarium keeper should never go on a hike without a container. He always finds something when he wanders outdoors with wide-awake senses.

The collector has profited considerably by the introduction of plastics. In tackle shops you can obtain plastic boxes for the storing of earthworms. Bait buckets, available in various sizes, do quite well for carrying terrarium animals home. Plastic bags can be stored in very small spaces. Avoid overheating, however— high temperatures can easily build up in closed plastic bags. For this reason, the linen sacks that were once standard equipment for holding animals should not be overlooked. They are best suited for transporting reptiles. Waterproof bags and backpacks should be opened at every stop so that sufficient fresh air can enter.

A net and forceps should not be missing on any expedition. Even on a walk through the town you for a small shovel as well as a keyhole saw. Here you see a suitable piece of branch, there some forest loam. If you wish to bring a delicate patch of moss home in one piece, carefully slip it into a flat can, similar to a sardine can. A box with wood shavings is useful for transporting suitable rocks. Of course, a car is needed to carry a bulky

Baby turtles (here a Red-eared Slider, Pseudemys scripta elegans) must be kept warm during transport and have access to breathable air. Photo by Dr. Herbert R. Axelrod.

may find earthworms after a rain or in the early morning on concrete and asphalt sidewalks and streets. These can be picked up with the forceps and stored in a flat worm can in a coat pocket.

You can often find use transport container of this kind.

OVER-WINTERING

Terrarium animals that in the wild normally spend the cold and food-poor times of year in hibernation do better in

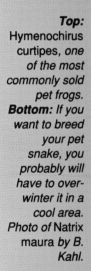

captivity if you over-winter them at cold temperatures, thereby reducing their metabolism to a minimum.

A wooden box is filled to a depth of about 30 centimeters with a mixture of moss, coarsely sifted forest soil, and chunks of peat. Diagonally inserted tiles or clay pipes help retain moisture better. A tight-closing wire-mesh cover protects against rats and mice and prevents the animals from escaping. The substrate should never dry out completely but should not be too moist. Sufficient humidity is important in the over-wintering room.

If you notice a certain degree of restlessness in the animals in late fall, the time for over-wintering has arrived. Place them in the box and observe whether they quickly burrow in. If they do not accept this opportunity to over-winter, then you must try it again later or continue to care for them in a heated room. The over-wintering room should be cold but free of frost. If possible, the animals should have

defecated before over-wintering, so they should not be fed beforehand. Only well-nourished animals can be trusted to the over-wintering box.

Over-wintering always presents a problem and often leads to disappointments. If you just wish to observe native terrarium animals temporarily, then you should release them at the location where they were captured early enough in the fall so they can find a place to spend the winter.

Although salamanders often are beautiful, they also are secretive and hard to observe in captivity. This Desmognathus ochrophaeus *was photographed by R. T. Zappalorti.*

Salamanders and Newts

Salamanders and newts are tailed amphibians. With their elongated forms and long tails, they differ conspicuously from frogs and toads. Their hind legs are not substantially longer than their front legs. They are not capable of hopping or jumping like frogs and toads. Most are ground-dwellers that are not especially adapted for climbing. When on land, they often crawl along slowly and sluggishly. During the time they spend on land they are almost always concealed, so we see them only rarely. They are capable, however, of temporarily switching to a faster pace. With increasing speed their running turns more and more into a sort of wriggling. The long tail makes possible this wriggling movement of the trunk. They present a curious appearance as they rapidly move off with the tail lashing back and forth. When in the water, salamanders proceed from crawling to crawl-swimming to wriggle-swimming as they move faster. When they want to go from the bottom to the water surface in order to get air, for example, the legs are pressed to the body; and the tail, its propulsive power usually increased by fins along the dorsal and ventral edges in aquatic species, moves side to side and propels the body rapidly forward. If they live on land, the tail usually does not have the fin-like form but instead is more rounded in cross-section.

In the newts, which are salamanders of the family Salamandridae that live on land for only part of their lives, the tail changes in form with the change in habits. We are thus able to tell by the form of the tail whether the particular animal was living on land or in the water. Newts, as is true of most salamanders in general, seek out the water only in the spring, during the breeding season. Their body then adapts to life in the water. The propulsive power of the laterally compressed, knife-like rowing tail is then increased by the growth of fins of varying height. The

Newts often are bred in captivity. This is a larval Triturus cristatus. Photo by M. Gilroy.

males of some species have a high and in some cases bizarrely serrated dorsal crest that serves to intimidate rivals when courting for the females. In the larvae, which hatch from the eggs in water,

Plethodon richmondi, *the Ravine Salamander, one of several small, slender woodland salamanders from the northeastern United States. Photo by W. B. Allen, Jr.*

in mind when keeping these animals.

KEEPING SALAMANDERS AND NEWTS

The terrestrial forms of salamanders and newts require a terrarium in which moist air prevails. All-glass or metal-framed aquaria are especially suitable. Not too fine gravel or soil, which must be replaced at intervals because of leaching and calcification, is covered with patches of moss under which the animals like to hide. Thick sheets of foam rubber, which become saturated with water and thereby provide moisture to the bottom and the air, are also suitable as a substrate. Press them in firmly, particularly when using a double layer, so that they cannot be as easily burrowed under by the animals (danger of drowning!). Cut out holes in the top layer to form shallow water holes.

Water the terrarium only enough that the patches of moss are not in standing water. It should be damp but not wet. Pieces of bark and flat moss-covered rocks serve as refuges.

adaptation to the aquatic way of life is particularly distinct. The high fin edges of their tails extend well onto the back. The legs, of which first the front and then the rear appear, are quite delicate. Large external gill tufts that serve as respiratory organs lend the animals an odd appearance. As the time of the transformation, or metamorphosis, to a land animal approaches, the gills and fin edges disappear and the internal breathing organs and skin assume the essential task of supplying oxygen. When the animals are in the terrestrial air-breathing stage they are quite capable of drowning under certain circumstances, particularly if they accidentally fall into deep water. This should be kept

Only toward evening or during rainy weather will you be able to see the animals. Earthworms and slugs often are simply thrown into the cage. You can of course also feed the animals individually with forceps. In springtime, fire salamanders *(Salamandra)* and newts need an area of water about 2 centimeters deep. It is best to transfer salamanders and newts, once they have gone into the water section, into a proper aquarium with relatively soft water. The water can be more than 10 centimeters deep in this tank, but the salamanders must have the opportunity to at least occasionally stick their heads out of the water. You can achieve this by introducing a thick bunch of *Elodea.* A sturdy bush of *Ludwigia* in a pot or a plant dish also gives the salamanders support when they want to rest and stick their heads out of the water to breathe. If you wish to install a larger area of land, a cork bridge fastened between the walls or a rock that protrudes above the water surface is suitable for the purpose. The corners of

the tank must remain open, however. If the salamanders struggle for a long time while trying to climb onto the land section, they can drown. This is especially true when they push against the cork from below in a corner. They do not consciously find the way to the land section, but rather only accidentally. A substrate of coarse sand or fine gravel makes it easier for the animals to walk.

In spring the males

Western North American specialties.
Top: Ensatinas, Ensatina eschscholtzii.
Bottom: A Giant Salamander, Dicamptodon ensatus.
Photos by K. Lucas, Steinhart Aquarium.

Egg mass of the Axolotl, Ambystoma mexicanum, *on elodea. Photo by L. Andres.*

begin to court the females. Erect, with fanning tail, they dance around the females. This graceful display is also accompanied by harmless bites. The male's cloaca is rounded like a pea at this time, extremely swollen. The male places the sperm on the bottom, where it is taken up by the female as she crawls over it. The female then attaches the eggs to aquatic plants. In many species each egg is individually wedged into the leaf of an aquatic plant *(Elodea, Ludwigia).* Once a fairly large number of eggs have been laid, either remove the adults or transfer the plants with the attached eggs to a special rearing tank; the adult newts are inveterate spawn-eaters. Keep the aquarium with the eggs completely free of snails and out of strong light. Salamander tanks are best placed in a north-facing window. After hatching, the larvae sink to the bottom or hang on the plants. Feeding is unnecessary in the first days of life; later offer infusoria and finely sieved daphnia. If daphnia are present in large numbers, however, they can do great damage to the larvae because there are also "predatory daphnia." The larvae grow rapidly and are soon able to devour, besides daphnia, small whiteworms and chopped tubifex. Do not try to rear too many larvae in one tank. At the time of transformation place the larvae in a tank with shallow water in which there is an easily climbed land section, such as a flat, properly shaped brick.

Once the animals have gone onto land they are transferred to a terrarium containing water only a few millimeters deep as well as a dense tangle of *Tradescantia* or approximately chestnut-sized pieces of brick. These hold the moisture very well, and the whiteworms that are regularly added creep around on them to be taken by the young newts. However, make sure that there are no blind-ended cracks among the pieces of brick in which the young newts could get caught. Once they have reached a size of 3 to 4 centimeters, you can increase the depth to 1 centimeter. Some will now occasionally enter the water and can also be fed there on small bloodworms and individual tubifex worms.

Although salamanders and newts are bottom-dwelling or ground-dwelling animals, they can easily escape from the cage. Most of them are able to climb glass panes, above all in the corners. If one uses an overhanging cover of metal with wire mesh, the animals will not be able to displace it. If you cover the cage with only a pane of glass, it is recommended that you glue small cubes of glass in the corners on the underside of the cover. Their corners must be well rounded so that the animals cannot injure themselves. A collar of cellophane or plastic film around the top rim of the aquarium prevents a displacement of the cover. If a wire-mesh cover is used, the plastic film should also be laid on top of it in order to maintain the humidity in the tank.

Elodea and similar plants often are used as egg-laying sites by salamanders and should always be available. Photo by L. Wischnath.

By changing the amount of area covered with plastic you can regulate the humidity.

For reasons of hygiene, newts are often kept in aquaria without substrates during the time they live in water. Such tanks are of course easier to keep clean because the bottom is regularly siphoned. The animals also find the food more easily in such a tank. They can crawl more easily on a substrate of fine gravel, which also more closely resembles the conditions they live under in nature. A disadvantage is that worms and midge larvae hide in the gravel, often going undetected and perhaps dying there and fouling the substrate. This can be remedied by the use of the suction devices available in aquarium shops.

NEWT SPECIES

Of the European newts, the most familiar is the Common or Smooth Newt *(Triturus vulgaris)*. It barely reaches 10 centimeters in length and is on the whole quite dainty. The high, undulating dorsal crest of the male merges into the tail without a clear break. The darkly spotted, flecked, and striped markings on the brown or olive ground color are quite attractive. The breeding attire of the male is striking with its fairly large blackish spots and the pearly, iridescent lateral stripe. After spawning the animals absolutely must be kept outside of the water. The skin then becomes duller

The Western or California Newt, Taricha torosa, *is a strikingly colored animal. Photo by A. Norman.*

15 centimeters and is recognized by its dark brown, almost blackish coloration and large black spots. The yolk-yellow, black-speckled undersides are unmistakable. The male is distinguished by a high, serrated crest during the breeding season; this is interrupted at the base of the tail. These are robust animals that can manage correspondingly large food animals. A pearl-colored stripe flashes on the tail.

Closely related to this species and just as large is the handsome Marbled Newt *(Triturus marmoratus)*, whose area of occurrence includes the Iberian Peninsula and central France. The fact that its blackish and green coloration is retained even after it changes to a

and more velvety.

The Palmate Newt *(Triturus helveticus)*, which is about the same size, is rarer and is limited to western Europe. In place of a crest, the male exhibits only a low ridge of skin but has a peculiar filament on the end of the tail and blackish, lobe-like "gloves" on the hind feet. It should also be kept in water in the spring.

The same is true of the large Crested Newt *(Triturus cristatus)*. It reaches a length of 13 to

Both the Smooth Newt (Triturus vulgaris, top) and the Palmate Newt (Triturus helveticus, bottom) have elaborate spawning rituals easily observed in the aquarium. Photo at top by B. Kahl, that at bottom by L. Wischnath.

terrestrial mode of life makes it especially sought after. The females and the highly prized juveniles additionally exhibit a reddish yellow dorsal line. The males are an imposing sight in breeding coloration. The high, continuous crest with alternating black and green markings is certainly not as bizarrely serrated as in the Crested Newt, but it is impressive because of its height and coloration. The Crested and Marbled Newts interbreed with each other. Some specimens of the Marbled Newt can be kept in water all year around at cool temperatures.

The most beautiful of the European newts is the Alpine Newt *(Triturus alpestris)*. The splendid orange-red underside stands out brilliantly against the blue-gray marbled back. Although no high dorsal crest adorns the breeding male, it does have a low, alternately yellow and black banded ridge of skin. The spotted sides gleam a magnificent blue. These are handsome animals, particularly in their aquatic coloration. The fact that the majority of specimens can be kept in water all year around if the water is cool enough makes them one of the most highly recommended newts. Particularly attractive is the northern Italian subspecies, *Triturus alpestris apuana*. Because of its small size (8 to 10 centimeters in length), it does well in fairly small aquaria (approximately 30 by 15 centimeters).

Also very well suited for keeping in the aquarium is

the Spanish Newt *(Triturus boscai)*, which occurs on the Iberian Peninsula. This small newt, which reaches a length of at most 9 centimeters, is very similar to the Common Newt. Small dark spots are present on a yellow-brown or olive ground color. The male lacks a crest but possesses a whitish tail tip. The food should not be too large, because large pieces seem to give these newts trouble. If the animals press far out of the water you should give them the opportunity to go on land. Once on land they hide themselves and then live in the same way

as the Common Newt.

Not much larger and also suitable for the aquarium is the Red-spotted Newt or Red Eft *(Notophthalmus viridescens)* from the eastern part of the United States. The olive-green aquatic coloration exhibits

Top: Triturus marmoratus, *the Marbled Newt. Photo by K. Lucas, Steinhart Aquarium.* *Bottom:* Triturus alpestris, *the Alpine Newt. Photo by L. Wischnath.*

Opposite:
Top: The Western Newt, Taricha torosa. Photo by K. Lucas, Steinhart Aquarium. *Bottom:* The Japanese Fire-bellied Newt, Cynops pyrrhogaster. Photo by B. Kahl.

A Red Eft, the terrestrial stage of the Red-spotted Newt, Notophthalmus viridescens. Photo by J. Dodd.

a delicate red and black speckling that reminds one of a pen and ink drawing. It takes on a red-brown color in the terrestrial form. In the very tumultuous mating ritual the male clasps the female with the hind legs in the shoulder area. The subspecies *Notophthalmus viridescens dorsalis,* the Broken-striped Newt, possesses two splendid broken red stripes on the back.

The Western Newt *(Taricha torosa)* from the southwestern part of the United States reaches a length of 16 to 18 centimeters. Its head is conspicuously broad and flat, the skin rough. The uniform black-brown to red-brown coloration is sharply set off from the yellow-orange of the underside. The males clasp the females from above during mating. In temperament this American is quiet and stays in the water a relatively long time, but it should always have the opportunity to go onto land.

From Japan comes the Japanese Fire-bellied Newt *(Cynops pyrrhogaster).* Although the back is almost black, the underside glows in magnificent red. Depending on its provenance, it is covered with varying numbers of fairly coarse or fine black spots. In the males, in particular, distinct humps bulge out in the ear region. The male is distinguished from the female by the shorter tail, which is more rounded on the end, and during the breeding season by the spherically swollen cloaca. The 10 to 12 centimeter animals are robust, quite voracious, and can be kept in the aquarium all the year around. There is no more suitable salamander than this Japanese species, which survives for decades in the aquarium and also reproduces there.

Just as long-lived

is the Rough Newt *(Pleurodeles waltl)* with a length of 20 to 25 centimeters. The head is conspicuously flat and somewhat toad-like. The grainy, warty skin of the trunk exhibits a gray-black marbling on a generally olive background. A row of brown-yellow warts on each side of

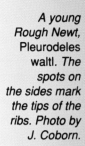

A young Rough Newt, Pleurodeles waltl. *The spots on the sides mark the tips of the ribs. Photo by J. Coborn.*

the back marks the ends of the ribs, which can be felt through the skin with strong finger pressure. The long, flattened tail reveals the propensity for the aquatic way of life. This newt can be kept constantly in the aquarium. This should be roomy because these newts, which come from the Iberian Peninsula and North Africa, are at times quite boisterous. During mating the male clasps the front legs of the female with his own from below. Both animals swim around for a long time joined together in this manner. The several hundred eggs normally produced are laid in clumps, not individually. This undemanding newt is extraordinarily productive. Although *Pleurodeles waltl*

is limited in Africa to parts of Morocco, *Pleurodeles poireti* occurs in Tunisia and Algeria. It is smaller, reaching a length of up to approximately 15 centimeters, and does not exhibit the yellow-brown to reddish "rib warts."

When we speak of "newts" and "salamanders" in the use of common names, this should not be considered a precise scientific manner of expression. The Alpine Salamander and the Fire Salamander, both of which live on land and have terrestrial adaptations, are classed with the salamanders, although they belong to the same family as the newts, Salamandridae. Their skin is coarser than that of aquatic-stage newts. The tail is round in cross-section, and there are no fins, dorsal crests, or foot webbings. Both of these salamanders can drown. The skin of the average newt is softer, its body more graceful, and the tail is never completely round even during the terrestrial part of its life cycle. They also spend part of the year in the water and move

there effortlessly and confidently.

The familiar Fire Salamander *(Salamandra salamandra)* is without doubt one of the most beautiful amphibians. Its absolutely distinctive combination of colors, the ease with which it can be kept, and its durability, as well as the diversity of its

The Fire Salamander, Salamandra salamandra. *Photo by B. Kahl.*

Top: The Fire Salamander, Salamandra salamandra. *Photo by M. Gilroy.* **Bottom:** *The Alpine Salamander,* Salamandra atra. *Photo by Ch. Vaucher, courtesy Dr. D. Terver, Nancy, France.*

markings, make it an extremely appealing specimen for the terrarium. The large area of occurrence extends from northern Germany to North Africa, from the Iberian Peninsula as far as Asia Minor. There are numerous described subspecies and a tremendous amount of variation in color pattern between localized populations.

The form of the Fire Salamander is quite coarse, the head broad. The parotoid glands are prominent, and longitudinal rows of glandular lumps extend along either side of the trunk. The velvet-yellow spots or stripes are sharply set off from the shiny black ground color. They can vary greatly in form and color. Rarely are specimens with orange-red spots found, but somewhat more

frequently seen are those in which the yellow coloration greatly predominates. These salamanders usually remain hidden during the day. On rainy days or toward dusk they leave their hiding places in order to hunt for worms, slugs,

The well-ventilated cage is sprayed in the evening. A shallow water container for the laying of the eggs is necessary in the spring. The larvae can be distinguished from newt larvae by a yellow spot at the base of each leg. They are found in early spring

isopods, and insects. Central European Fire Salamanders attain a length of about 20 centimeters; other subspecies can reach 8 to 10 centimeters longer.

Keep these salamanders in correspondingly large terraria that are furnished with an abundance of moss and rocks. Hiding places must be present.

in quiet coves of woodland streams and ditches. It is easy to rear them with daphnia, whiteworms, and aquatic insects. Rearing them is a fascinating activity because you cannot tell from looking at the larvae which coloration they will later have. Furthermore, the newly transformed young salamanders are quite

A large and brightly colored specimen of the Tiger Salamander, Ambystoma tigrinum. Photo by R. T. Zappalorti.

Axolotls, Ambystoma mexicanum, occur in many colors, but the gray phase with dark stippling perhaps is most common. Photo by K. Paysan.

charming animals. In winter these salamanders should be given the customary period of dormancy.

The Alpine Salamander *(Salamandra atra)* is smaller (up to 15 centimeters) and more delicate than the Fire Salamander. The uniform glossy black coloration, which is not interrupted by markings of any kind, gives these charming animals the appearance of ebony. The parotoid glands as well as the glandular lateral lumps of the trunk are more distinct than those of the Fire Salamander. The nimble Alpine Salamander occurs only in alpine regions.

It does quite well when the terrarium is well-ventilated and the furnishings (limestone, soil, moss, and ferns), as far as possible, come from the place the animal was collected. It does not require a water container; spraying the cage in the evening is sufficient. During the evening the salamanders hunt for earthworms and slugs.

AMERICAN SALAMANDERS

Even larger than the Fire Salamander is the Tiger Salamander *(Ambystoma tigrinum),* which is widely distributed in the United States. The specimens offered on the

market are generally about 15 centimeters long; however, the species grows to a length of 25 centimeters or more. A yellow-olive marbling consisting of large, irregularly shaped spots and/or stripes (in most subspecies) stands out sharply against a black background. The markings and coloration vary considerably. The water section of the tank can be 3 to 6 centimeters deep depending on the size of the animals. The land section should contain well-rounded flat rocks and patches of moss plus suitable hiding places. This salamander feeds on earthworms, slugs, and insects. The larvae of some subspecies grow to a very large size and do not leave the water. They remain in the larval stage and reproduce without taking on adult characteristics.

Neoteny—which is the proper term for a persistent larval stage of

Top: The Spotted Salamander, Ambystoma maculatum. Photo by B. Kahl. **Bottom:** The Marbled Salamander, Ambystoma opacum. Photo by J. Dommers.

A Dusky Salamander, Desmognathus fuscus. *Photo by J. Dodd.*

this kind—is most familiar in the Axolotl (*Ambystoma mexicanum*) of Mexico, which does not metamorphose under normal conditions. We often find 20 to 25 centimeters Axolotls, and they are said to reach a length of almost 30 centimeters. There are black, yellowish, gray-black spotted, and white specimens. In albinos the bright red external gills produce a unique contrast as a result of the blood showing through the skin. The fat head with the broad larval mouth, the small eyes, and the feathery, protruding gill bundles, which flick like the ears of a horse in summer pasture, produce a truly strange appearance.

Axolotls are kept in large aquaria with clear water and abundant plant growth (*Elodea*). They greedily eat lean meat cut into strips, small fishes, worms, and other food animals. Breeding and rearing are easy, except that the small larvae are quite voracious. If many specimens are kept in a tank and are not fed enough, they will mutilate each other's external gills.

The Spotted Salamander (*Ambystoma maculatum*), which occurs in eastern North America, does not attain the imposing size of the Tiger Salamander or Axolotl, but nevertheless grows to a length of slightly more than 20 centimeters. On a black background are two rows of round yellow or orange spots that give the animal a quite colorful appearance. Water is sought out only for breeding in the spring. The rest of the year this salamander lives concealed on land in moist environments under rocks and wood.

The Marbled Salamander *(Ambystoma opacum)* also leads a hidden lifestyle. Its small size (10 to 12 centimeters), its brilliant coloration, and its ease of keeping make it the most suitable terrarium salamander of the North American species discussed here. Silvery white hourglass-shaped dorsal bands gleam against a black background. These handsome fellows look as if they were lacquered and remind one of enamel art. An aquatic tank is

unnecessary. They do not require as much moisture as most of the *Ambystoma* species with which they share a large range in the eastern part of the United States. Thick layers of moss on a bed of fairly coarse sand or gravel give them the opportunity to excavate their own hiding places. Pieces of bark are also accepted. They try to find the most concealed hiding places. For example, they tunnel under the tightly clinging moss growing on a rock, and you could search a long time for the supposed escapees before finding them in the terrarium. Once they have become

One of the most striking of North American salamanders is the Red Salamander, Pseudotriton ruber. Photo by R. T. Zappalorti.

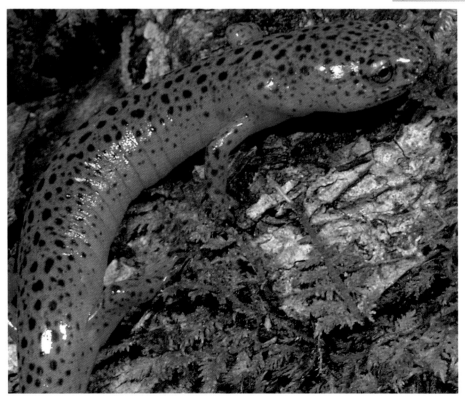

Several color varieties and subspecies of Red Salamander occur. This is the black-chinned P. r. schnecki. Photo by Dr. S. A. Minton.

found on the shiny gray-brown back. The light belly skin is peculiarly transparent. These slender, extremely agile animals usually live hidden near flowing water, and high humidity is very much to their liking. To make them feel at home, coarse gravel and well-rounded rocks from a stream bed are covered with patches of moss. These elegant animals also like to visit the shallow water section. Nimbly and with great skill they capture worms, slugs, millipedes, moths, spiders, and flies. Cat-like, they stalk flying insects before seizing them in a flash with their powerful jaws and slipping away between rocks and small ferns in the twilight. The cage must be particularly well covered because these salamanders are excellent escape artists. If you must catch one for some reason, carefully drive it into a soft net. The fast, slippery creatures are very difficult to catch with the hand.

acclimated, their heads dart out of the moss burrows at feeding time to capture earthworms, slugs, and other animals. If the cage is equipped with a red light, you can observe them hunting for food in the evening or at night. The egg clutch is laid in a hollow in the moss. This must be flooded after a while so that the larvae can hatch. Rearing them is a real pleasure, as more lovable aquarium inhabitants scarcely exist for the newt and salamander fancier.

Completely different in its habits is the relatively elongated Dusky Salamander *(Desmognathus fuscus)*. It is perhaps the most familiar and widespread lungless salamander in North America. The coloration of the 10 to 12 centimeters adults is relatively drab. Dark speckles and traces of paired light spots are

Nothing short of conspicuous is the about 15 centimeters Red Salamander *(Pseudotriton ruber)*, which occurs in the eastern United States. The gleaming coral-red back and sides covered with small black dots make it reminiscent of a rod of red sealing wax. Setting off the red is the golden color of the iris—you cannot take your eyes off it. In some animals, above all in old age, the conspicuous bright coloration becomes more flesh-colored. The subspecies *Pseudotriton ruber schencki* (Black-chinned Red Salamander) seems to exhibit the bright velvet red color the longest. This unique coloration makes up for the shy temperament of the exquisite animals. In the wild they live hidden under rocks and patches of moss by clear streams and also like to go into the water. With this in mind, arrange the cage as follows: one or two rows of hollow bricks laid side by side are covered with rod-shaped stones, such as one finds in streambeds, laid crosswise on top of one another; on top is placed a layer of moss or a flat stone to form a seal. The water section is thickly planted with *Elodea* or moss. These slimy, smooth, expert wrigglers like to press into the narrowest cracks and avoid light, so they should be disturbed as little as possible. Wait until evening before giving them their food (earthworms, daphnia, bloodworms). Animals of this kind should not be touched unnecessarily with the hands. Moving them in a

The Spring Salamander, Gyrinophilus porphyriticus, is closely related to the Red Salamander though duller in color. Photo by G. Dingerkus.

A Slimy
Salamander,
Plethodon
glutinosus.
This "species"
is now known
to be a
complex of at
least 13
genetically
distinct types,
each named
as a full
species,
ranging over
the eastern
United States.
Photo by G.
Dingerkus.

soft net will do the least amount of damage.

The Spring Salamander *(Gyrinophilus porphyriticus)*, also from the eastern United States, has similar habits. It is striking because of its size (up to about 20 centimeters) and its often salmon-red coloration. As its name indicates, it likes very clean, cold spring water.

The Slimy Salamander *(Plethodon glutinosus)* of the eastern United States is conspicuous because of its slender form. The approximately 15 centimeter salamander is black, dusted with fine blue-white spots above, its underside lighter, more grayish. It does not live in water, but instead is found in moist forest ravines. You should occasionally spray the cage with water. It feeds on worms and insects. Slimy Salamanders do not lay their eggs in water, but rather under rocks or patches of moss. The young are hatched fully developed and look like miniatures of the parents, never undergoing an aquatic stage.

The Two-lined Salamander *(Eurycea bislineata)*, from the northeastern part of the United States, prefers the aquatic way of life. In a moderate sized tank furnished like a stream bank, it will wriggle in the shallow water between fairly large, well-rounded stones. This conspicuously

slender, slippery, and quite lively salamander has a creamy tan to brownish back outlined by a broad black lateral stripe on each side, while the · belly is uniformly bright yellow. This very common, quite elegant looking salamander reaches a length of only 8 to 10 centimeters and feeds on worms, aquatic insects, and crustaceans, as well as insects and spiders.

Top: Eurycea bislineata. *Photo by W. B. Allen, Jr.* ***Bottom:*** Pseudoeurycea belli. *Photo by R. S. Simmons.*

Frogs and Toads

Frogs and toads do not have tails after transformation. Their larvae, tadpoles, of which the majority hatch from eggs in water, move through the water by wriggling with the aid of a well-developed propulsive tail. Fine horny teeth enable tadpoles to grasp algae and protozoans from rocks, wood, and leaves and to occasionally feed on living or dead animals and thereby meet their enormous food requirements. The majority of tadpoles are primarily or exclusively vegetarian and can be reared without difficulty in captivity with various prepared foods. First their hind legs and then their front legs appear (front legs first in salamander larvae). The fin crests of the tail gradually disappear before the tail itself is resorbed. Transformation, or metamorphosis, takes place before the tail is completely lost. The powerful hind legs let the tailless frog or toad move in a completely different manner from the crawling salamander. The four legs are not used alternately, but simultaneously. The long and powerful hind legs propel the body forward and upward, so frogs and toads hop and jump. The treefrogs (*Hyla*) and true frogs (*Rana*) are particularly specialized jumpers. They therefore need an appropriately high cage so that their muscular legs do not atrophy. The jumping power is proportional to the length of the legs. The short-legged toads confine themselves more to hopping and creeping or running. In frogs and toads that live in the water temporarily or permanently, the hind feet exhibit more or less strongly developed webs. The skin of most frogs is adapted to absorbing water; toads, however, can withstand temporary dryness. A certain amount of humidity should therefore be maintained in the cage. A water container belongs in a terrarium for frogs and toads, and you should never dispense with a daily spraying.

TRUE FROGS

The European Edible Frog (*Rana esculenta*) inhabits virtually all of Europe. The combination

A Leopard Frog, Rana pipiens *or a closely related species. Photo by Lacey.*

of green, brown, yellow, gold-bronze, and black, in the majority of specimens with the green ground color predominating, makes this one of the most attractive frogs. This aquatic frog reaches a body length of up to 9 centimeters; males remain somewhat smaller. Especially appealing are very young specimens. These initially quite unruly fellows must first be acclimated. As much as they like to wait for prey in the full sun on the bank of a body of water, the water is their true element. It also provides them with shelter when they detect danger. The well-developed webs on the hind feet mark them as powerful swimmers. You should equip the cage with a fairly large water section into which they can jump at any time. They do this quick as a flash, but after a while a watchful pair of eyes surfaces here and there. If you add a bit of peat to the water, the animals will feel better hidden and more secure. They will soon become acclimated and will turn to the keeper with eager anticipation when he approaches the cage. This behavior is dictated by their almost insatiable appetite. No prey capable of being seized seems too large for them; they swallow unbelievably large food animals and by no means limit themselves to insects such as flies and grasshoppers. Even young mice are seized by the broad mouth, which extends to under the clearly visible tympanum, and swallowed down the insatiable gullet. The choice of food for these predators, which do not shrink from cannibalism, provides no difficulty.

A cage for frogs of this kind of course may be equipped only with patches of moss and robust, resistant plants. Delicate plants are demolished in short order by these rowdy animals. Additionally, they do not behave exactly gently with one another. They often fight stubbornly over desirable food animals, and only their comparable size prevents them from consuming their rivals. Keep only specimens of about the same size together and you will then be able to derive real pleasure from the temperamental fellows.

The European Grass Frog or Common Frog *(Rana temporaria),* which is widely distributed in Europe, belongs to the "brown frogs." In contrast to the "water frogs," it does not stay in the water except during the very early breeding season, but instead inhabits open woods and fields. The brown coloration at times has a reddish tinge and exhibits black speckling. The coloration is extremely variable, some specimens being gray with black speckling. There is a black, ribbon-like stripe in the ear region. When fully grown, this relatively

A mating pair of Moor Frogs, Rana arvalis. Photo by L. Wischnath.

The Large Harlequin Frog, Pseudis paradoxa.

placid and long-lived frog reaches a length of 10 centimeters.

The Moor Frog *(Rana arvalis)* of Europe has unfortunately become rarer with the reduction of moorlands. It grows only slightly larger than 6 centimeters and is distinguished from the Grass Frog by the more pointed snout, the unspotted belly, and the fairly large, sharply protruding heel tubercle. Many specimens have a conspicuous light dorsal line that varies in coloration from brown to gray. Particularly attractive are gray specimens with fine black spotting and striped markings that resemble an India ink drawing. These lively animals are more active than the Grass Frog and do quite well in the terrarium.

The Australian Spotted Grass Frog *(Limnodynastes tasmaniensis)* is to some extent a match for the European Grass Frog in toughness and voracity, but at a maximum length of about 5 centimeters it remains considerably smaller. Some specimens exhibit a light yellow central stripe on the gray-brown, dark-spotted back. During the day this frog likes to hide, lying in wait for anything it can overpower. It likes water and is therefore best kept in an aqua-terrarium. Plant the land section, consisting of peat bricks, with fairly small *Calamus* species, fairly large *Tradescantia,* or other fairly tough plants. Hiding places are constructed of suitably cut out pieces of peat or sections of bark. In the water section, roots and pieces of peat give the animals the opportunity to hide. At feeding time they rush out and snatch up the food. From worms to insects, they take everything directly from forceps once they have become acclimated. In the struggle for food, smaller members of their kind are sometimes grabbed, so take care that cannibalism does not occur when the feeding reflex is triggered. Supplementary heating of the cage is unnecessary in a heated room, since the animals certainly can tolerate temporary temperatures as low as 10°C (50°F). They start croaking at a very young age. A peculiarity of their reproduction is the construction of a bubblenest at the water surface in which the eggs develop.

The Large Harlequin Frog *(Pseudis paradoxa)* from South America is totally aquatic. Keep it in an aquarium with cushions of floating plants or aquatic plants that blanket the water's surface. The olive-green spotted frogs lie hidden in the plants or hang suspended among them. The nostrils and the upwardly pointed eyes protrude above the water surface. As soon as a food animal is spotted, the community suddenly comes to life. They even take pieces of food from forceps once they are acclimated. All in all, they are comical fellows. The

A Spring Peeper, Pseudacris crucifer. Until recently this little frog was put in the genus Hyla. Photo by W. Mudrack.

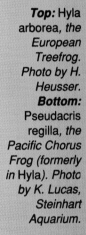

Top: Hyla arborea, *the European Treefrog. Photo by H. Heusser.* ***Bottom:*** Pseudacris regilla, *the Pacific Chorus Frog (formerly in* Hyla*). Photo by K. Lucas, Steinhart Aquarium.*

of the tropical world. They generally live in trees and shrubs, their splendidly developed climbing ability enabling them to climb up even smooth branches and leaves. With the pad-like discs on the ends of their toes they can adhere to almost any surface. In captivity they must be given the opportunity to climb and jump, otherwise the powerful muscles of the legs rapidly atrophy. Tall, airy cages with branches and climbing plants agree with them. A rear wall of small, smooth beech branches gives them even greater opportunity to climb and perch, and then they will not hang as often on the panes and soil them. A water container is visited only to lay the eggs, so a regular spraying of the cage is sufficient. The cage should not be completely damp and never dripping wet. Ample ventilation is extremely important. As food, all insects that can be managed by the generally relatively

fact that the frogs are about 7 centimeters long but the tadpoles can reach a length of 25 centimeters has given them the scientific name meaning "paradoxical" and also led to the common name Shrinking Frog.

TREEFROGS AND REEDFROGS

The several hundred known species of treefrogs (family Hylidae) and reedfrogs (Hyperoliidae) are distributed over much

small species are suitable.

The European Treefrog *(Hyla arborea)* inhabits an extensive area from Scandinavia to Sicily and from Spain as far as the Urals. Unfortunately, its habitat is becoming greatly restricted by the spread of civilization. The rich green of the back is not interrupted by markings of any kind. The vocal pouch of the male is dark and is distended like a ball when calling. Only during breeding season do these up to 5 centimeters frogs leave the branches and seek out the water. They are extraordinarily well camouflaged, and you can only find them on reeds, for example, after a long search. In summer they are often found far from water. In hot sunshine they are found, for example, in brambles and hedges.

The Pacific Treefrog *(Hyla regilla)* from western North America is capable of great changes of coloration. The brown or green back has dark stripes and/or spotted markings. The legs may have transverse dark stripes.

More slender and somewhat longer (6 cm) is the eastern North American Green Treefrog *(Hyla cinerea)*, which exhibits a broad yellowish white stripe on the sides. In the northern specimens this stripe may not be as distinct. The solid green back may have scattered golden freckles.

The Green Treefrog, Hyla cinerea. *Photo by A. Norman.*

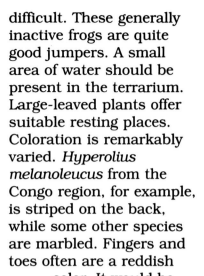

The Australian
Green or
Dumpy
Treefrog,
Litoria
caerulea.
Photo by K.
Lucas,
Steinhart
Aquarium.

A giant in comparison is the Australian Green Treefrog or White's Treefrog *(Hyla caerulea)*. This rich green treefrog from northern and eastern Australia reaches a length of about 10 centimeters and accordingly requires correspondingly large food animals: worms, caterpillars, insects, and spiders, even nestling mice. Do not be frightened by the baying call. Like

difficult. These generally inactive frogs are quite good jumpers. A small area of water should be present in the terrarium. Large-leaved plants offer suitable resting places. Coloration is remarkably varied. *Hyperolius melanoleucus* from the Congo region, for example, is striped on the back, while some other species are marbled. Fingers and toes often are a reddish color. It would be impossible to discuss here the diversity of individual species and their variability. If you find a reedfrog on a dealer's price list, you should ask about the markings and coloration if you want to be certain of obtaining especially attractively marked and colored specimens.

other Australian treefrogs it is often placed in a separate genus, *Litoria*.

The reedfrogs *(Hyperolius,* family Hyperoliidae or Rhacophoridae), treefrogs from Africa that grow to a length of several centimeters, attract notice because of their particularly striking colors and markings and also because of the variability of the same, which makes identification extremely

The South American treefrogs and African reedfrogs, in keeping with the climatic conditions that exist there, require constantly high temperature and humidity. Because they continue to eat with the same appetite in the winter, obtaining food for them is more difficult than with temperate treefrogs. An exception is the Marsupial Treefrog *(Gastrotheca marsupiata)* from western South America. This treefrog, which is brown or green with dark lichenose markings, reaches a length of 6 to 7 centimeters. It is somewhat clumsy and inactive. Fully grown animals are incapable of climbing up and adhering to glass side panes of the terrarium. Consequently, they do not smear the glass. By installing branches covered with climbing plants, epiphytes, and orchid baskets, you give the animals the opportunity to climb. Their voracity causes them to snap at everything that moves or is moved before their mouths. For this reason they are very easily acclimated to feeding from forceps, but then they become even more inactive and placid. They accept almost anything even remotely edible, so it is not difficult to give them chopped, raw, lean hamburger mixed with a calcium supplement and small amounts of vitamins in the wintertime. Precisely because they are so sluggish, you should try to give them live fresh food in the cage that they must catch themselves by jumping. Then they can even become quite lively! If you put in butterflies, you'll no longer be able to

recognize your pets—with incredible liveliness they will hunt the butterflies until the last one has landed in their swollen bellies.

In addition to their attractive appearance, these frogs have many other merits, including becoming quite tame and trusting. They wait for feeding time every day in the same spot and literally

A rather plain reedfrog, Hyperolius fusciventris. Photo by W. Mudrack.

Gastrotheca marsupiata, the Marsupial Treefrog. Several almost identical species are available in the hobby. Photo by O. Klee.

allow themselves to be stuffed. Although this hand-feeding permits good control of the food intake, it may also lead to unhealthy obesity. They like to sit in the leaf cups of large bromeliads, and they only need open water when the time comes to release their larvae. These hatch in a brood pouch on the female's back, the slit-like opening of which can be clearly seen. The pouch bulges visibly when the eggs are inserted. The larvae can be reared with prepared foods. It is a wonderful sight when a number of these frogs sit in a row on a branch or when they peek out with their gold-rimmed eyes from the cup of a bromeliad. When something is not to their liking they retreat backward into the cup. If the forceps come near with a grasshopper or some other piece of food, however, they rise farther and farther out of the depths of the cup before finally seizing the tidbit with smacking lips. The fact that they do not need any heating of their cage in winter as long as normal room temperatures are maintained is an additional merit of this commendable frog.

HORNED FROGS AND OTHERS

A highly distinctive frog is the handsome Ornate Horned Frog (Ceratophrys *ornata).* With a length of about 15 centimeters, this species, which is imported from South America, is considerably smaller than some of its relatives, but its form nevertheless gives it an extremely imposing appearance. If you look at one of these frogs from the front, it appears to consist of only the shapeless, bumpy head and gigantic mouth, from which the broad back falls away to the rear. The powerful mouth and the pop-eyes crowned with peculiar pointed folds of skin, as well as the enormous vocal pouch, complete the simultaneously queer as well as threatening image of an insatiable, predatory eater. If it feels threatened, it inflates itself with air, and under certain circumstances it attacks even fairly large opponents, grunting and hissing all the while. It has a vise-like bite aided by tooth-like bony fangs and lets go only reluctantly. It does, however, become acclimated to its keeper with time and even allows itself to be taken without resistance from its hiding place and put in place for feeding.

The magnificent black, green, red, and brown coloration and markings unfortunately usually remain hidden from the observer because of the cryptic nocturnal habits. This powerful burrower digs itself into the loose peat substrate up to its eyes; it can completely plough up the substrate in a single night. If a food animal, no matter how large, comes within reach

A young Ornate Horned Frog, Ceratophrys ornata. *With age the head seems to become proportionately larger, eventually making the frog seem to be all mouth.* Photo by J. Wines.

of its powerful jaws, the broad mouth will suddenly spring open, and the worm, insect, mouse, or frog will disappear into the capacious maw. All of its strength and power lie in these powerful, threatening instruments of feeding, and it is uncanny what a horned frog can devour. Like a porcelain idol it crouches motionless in the twilight. You just cannot take your eyes off this peculiar, colorful creature. It likes the humid warmth of its Brazilian-Argentine homeland. Cater to its virtually subterranean habits by installing a 10 to 12 centimeters deep layer of peat or forest loam. The water container must be large enough to completely hold it for the nightly bath.

Because of its voracity and inclination to cannibalize, you should keep it only with others of its kind of about the same size—or preferably alone.

In contrast, the Dwarf Horned Frog *(Odontophrynus americanus)*, which also comes from South America, is a midget. It reaches a length of only 4 centimeters and has neither the splendid coloration nor the curious pointed horns of skin on the eyelids, so in appearance it cannot rival its large cousin.

The European Spadefoot *(Pelobates fuscus)* lives just as cryptically in loose sandy soils. Few of these 6 to 8 centimeters toads of the family Pelobatidae are seen in terraria. Rearing

Pelobates fuscus is the spadefoot toad of Europe. In North America the spadefoots belong to the genus Scaphiopus but are similar in appearance to Pelobates. Photo by G. Baumgart, courtesy Dr. D. Terver, Nancy, France.

their giant larvae, which reach a length of 10 centimeters or more, is an interesting activity. Feed them on finely chopped earthworms, lean meat, aquatic plants, and prepared food. Newly transformed Spadefoots, with their dark speckled markings and their red mottling on a light ground color, are quite attractive. With the aid of a horny digging tubercle or "spade" on each hind foot, the animals burrow into the ground extremely fast. They are difficult to keep for any period of time, so you should eventually release them at the site where they were collected.

The fire-bellied toads (*Bombina*), which are among the most comical terrarium animals of all, have completely different habits. They are highly recommended for the beginner because of their small size (only about 5 centimeters in length), as well as their unusual liveliness and durability. There are two European species. The Fire-bellied Toad *(Bombina bombina)* has a red-spotted

underside. The Yellow-bellied Toad (*Bombina variegata*) has a yellow-spotted underside. The red or yellow is interrupted by gray-black or blue-gray spots. The back in both species is an inconspicuous dark gray to light gray and exhibits darker spots and warts. These quite lively animals are very closely bound to water. With spread hind legs they hang at the surface of ponds, ditches, and pools, diving quickly at any sign of danger and reaching the safety of the bottom mud in seconds thanks to the large webs on the hind feet. If you surprise them on land at some distance from the water, they press themselves close to the ground and turn the margins of their bodies and their legs somewhat upward so that the warning coloration of the

The Oriental Fire-bellied Toad, Bombina orientalis, often is available in pet shops. Photo by Dr. H. Grier.

belly becomes visible. Their initial shyness quickly subsides in captivity, and soon they will swim up rapidly to greedily accept the food, from worms to insects. The squabbles that take place during feeding are very amusing to watch. The swimming space should not be too small and should be well planted with *Elodea.* A peat brick or a smoothed-off tile is sufficient for the land section. To catch them, approach cautiously from below with a net, since the always-alert eyes are usually directed upward. The unique melodic call of the male is never disturbing in the house.

Totally adapted to an aquatic way of life and completely dependent on this element are the African clawed or underwater frogs *(Xenopus).* They never leave the water voluntarily. When the bodies of water in which they live dry up during long droughts, they survive until the next rainfall by burrowing into the substrate. Their hind legs are heavy, with large webbed feet that propel the body rapidly through the water. It looks very peculiar when they swim backward. They voraciously fall upon everything that they can handle: fishes, worms, crustaceans, insects. They quickly become adjusted to the keeper, their upwardly pointed eyes quickly spotting the forceps with the pieces of food, which they hurriedly snatch up. In this manner you can easily feed them in the wintertime with pieces of meat or fish. The long, powerful hind legs are only used for propulsion, but the shorter front legs are used for control and for stuffing prey into

A Smooth Clawed Frog, Xenopus laevis. Notice the papillae around the vent that are typical of females. Photo by G. Dibley.

the mouth. Some of the toes have small black, horny claws. These often quite boisterous creatures need a fairly large swimming area if several of them are kept in the same tank. They like to rest on tangles of roots or robust aquatic plants. The water level should be high enough that they can effortlessly reach the surface when they stand diagonally in the water, their favorite position. Despite their provenance from central and southern Africa, high temperatures are not absolutely necessary for keeping them in aquaria. They are quite active at a temperature of 19 to 25°C

(66–77°F).

Their larvae are very peculiarly shaped and, because of their long "feelers" and their transparency, resemble to some extent the glass catfish. They feed on plankton and in captivity are initially fed with the finest well-sieved and soaked stinging nettle powder and just as finely pulverized prepared vegetable foods, which they swirl into their mouths.

The smooth gray-brown back of the Smooth or Common Clawed Frog *(Xenopus laevis)* generally exhibits a blackish pattern, but the coloration can grow much paler or become more distinct depending on the lighting conditions. The mating call consists of peculiar trilling and ticking sounds. The females (about 8 to 9 centimeters long) are larger than the males.

The dwarf clawed frogs *(Hymenochirus curtipes* and *Hymenochirus boettgeri,* among others) are only about 3 to 4 centimeters long and can be kept in fairly small aquaria. It is extremely amusing to watch their activities as they busily paddle around, disappearing hurriedly here and there in a crack between roots and rocks, before just as suddenly popping up somewhere else. If a fairly large fish approaches, they flatten the already flat body even more, but lift up the edges of their bodies and their slightly bent limbs. In this concave-backed posture they wait on the bottom of the tank until the presumed enemy has disappeared. They like thick carpets of plants in which to find protection and cover. Their larvae also filter the water, but live principally on animal food; at first they take infusoria, then the smallest brine shrimp, and then small daphnia.

TOADS

The true toads *(Bufo)* are represented in virtually all parts of the world except Australia and the Pacific Islands. Superstition and prejudice have brought them much persecution over the centuries. That they are poisonous is not the only defamation of character. To be sure, their warty skin is rich in glands, and the large parotoid glands

One of the most commonly kept and bred frogs is the tiny Hymenochirus curtipes, *the Dwarf Clawed Frog from Africa. Photo by Dr. H. Grier.*

behind the eyes bulge out. Their secretions, like those of certain salamanders, can cause irritation of the mucous membranes; the conjunctiva of the eye, in particular, exhibits a severe reaction when exposed to this slime. The animals are not, however, literally "venomous." After *any* handling of *any* amphibian you should always thoroughly wash your hands. Every keeper of amphibians should make this a rule!

night they occasionally like to sit in a water bath. Because the majority of toads are crepuscular animals, you can keep them in enclosed terraria. In the middle of the cage, prepare an open space that can be watched over from the covered hiding place. For feeding they will then rapidly appear at the feeding place prepared. It is really an amusing sight when several toads sit around a food dish and with their tongues open up a rapid fire on a small mound of mealworms or fly maggots. Earthworms, slugs, insects, and spiders are taken with special relish. Toads become acclimated very well, and soon each has its favorite place in the terrarium.

Toads are extraordinarily lovable animals. The nature of their skin indicates that they tolerate more dryness than do other amphibians, so you should accordingly keep them relatively dry. Regular spraying of the cage with warm water provides for sufficient humidity. This is best done in the evening at feeding time when the toads become active. At

The most common European toad is the Common Toad (*Bufo bufo*). Males reach a length of 8 centimeters, females up to 13 centimeters. Most specimens are an inconspicuous olive-green or brown color, but attractive rust-red tinted animals also occur. Newly transformed toadlets of the rust-red color are comical, handsome little fellows. The Common Toad ranges through almost all of Europe. In southern Europe it is replaced by

The European Common Toad, Bufo bufo, *has figured greatly in literature and legend.*

the subspecies *Bufo bufo spinosus*, which grows considerably larger (up to 20 centimeters) and develops thorny warts as an adult. In the spring Common Toads are found in large numbers in all imaginable accumulations of water. During the rest of the year, however, they live hidden during the day and are content with little moisture. As is true of other toads, never keep them wet. Above all, regularly check to see whether the hiding place that is always used has not become too wet through the secretions of the toad.

Without doubt one of the most attractive toads is the Green Toad *(Bufo viridis)*. Its range in central and southern Europe is unfortunately not very extensive, but they are encountered more frequently than the Common Toad during the day as well as outside the breeding season in or by water. The males often reveal themselves through their characteristic trilling. Up to 10 centimeters in length, these animals are relatively lively and are good swimmers. On an olive-gray background stand large green isolated islands of spots and small red warts. In North African Green Toads the bright green spots stand out on an almost white background. They are truly splendid animals!

The most comical and, in temperament, the most lovable toad is the Natterjack Toad *(Bufo calamita)*, which inhabits a wide belt from the Iberian Peninsula to western Russia. These toads are no match for the Green Toad in the beauty of the markings and colorations—they are olive-green to brown above with dark speckles and a yellowish central stripe. In addition to the usual charms and good qualities of toads that recommend them for keeping in the terrarium, the Natterjack also has lively, comical movements. Because the hind legs are relatively short, this 6 to 8 centimeters toad runs more than it hops. It really is a very funny sight to see these animals scurry away. Very young, newly transformed Natterjacks produce an especially comical effect. They really do scurry about at random like young mice, and they also climb relatively well for a toad, often tumbling over one another in their haste to escape. A charming sight! Whoever has had the opportunity to keep this toad in the terrarium will prefer it to many more exotic species. They are frequently found burrowing in areas with loose and dry soil conditions, and they should be given the opportunity to do this in the terrarium as well.

Of the African toads, the 12 centimeter Berber Toad *(Bufo mauritanicus)*, whose range is limited to North Africa, is offered on the market from time to time. It exhibits red-brown or black-brown, dark-edged spots on a light-brown background.

The Leopard Toad *(Bufo regularis)* is striking because of its large tympanum. In North Africa

Bufo viridis, the Green Toad, is one of the more colorful species of a rather dully-colored genus. Photo by B. Kahl.

it grows to a length of about 9 centimeters and is a rather plain light brown in color. South African specimens, in contrast, exhibit a quite attractive red-brown coloration with large, almost square spots.

Bufo calamita, the Natterjack Toad. Photo by H. Heusser.

Of the large number of North American toads, one, the small Oak Toad *(Bufo quercicus)*, from the southeastern portion of the United States, stands out in particular. It lives on the ground in pine woods and, at a size of 2.5 to 3.5 centimeters, is one of the midgets of the toad kingdom. Dark brown to blackish spots decorate a gray-brown background. Noteworthy is its chirping voice.

In the southwestern United States lives the American Green Toad *(Bufo debilis)*, which, at a size of 3.5 to 5 centimeters, can be considered one of the smaller toads. This relatively lively little toad is quite attractive, with dark mottling on a greenish background.

The Great Plains Toad *(Bufo cognatus)* is found from northern Mexico to southwestern Canada. It is a quite active and comical species that reaches a length of 5 to 9 centimeters, prefers drier conditions, and feeds mainly on insects and similar food animals. The rather blunt head with the short snout completes the comical impression that young animals, in particular, impart. When they tackle their food animals, the effect is even funnier. On a gray, brownish, or greenish background is a checkerboard pattern of light-bordered greenish, olive, or dark gray spots.

From South America comes the quite handsome 12-centimeter Sand Toad *(Bufo arenarum)*. The brown, dark-speckled coloration is relatively inconspicuous. They require warmth and large food animals: large grasshoppers, mealworms, newborn mice, and so forth.

The Marine Toad *(Bufo marinus)* is an attraction even in zoos. These toads, which are imported mostly from South America but also from Central America, reach a length of 20 centimeters or more. It is a prodigious eater that can swallow even fully grown mice. In addition to normal brown-flecked specimens, there are also very attractive light- and dark-flecked animals. This goliath is impressive not only because of its size, but also because of the powerful angled head. The eyes are somewhat roofed over by bone, and corresponding ridges of skin intensify the already peculiar expression. One can clearly see the individual pores in the very large parotoid glands in the ear region. These are inactive, good-natured animals that need large amounts of food.

REARING YOUNG FROGS AND TOADS

Today it is no longer difficult to rear the larvae of various frogs and toads. The development of excellent prepared foods for tropical fishes has also relieved the keeper of tadpoles of many concerns. Furthermore, these modern prepared types of food are very specialized—depending on need they have either predominantly vegetable or

Bufo regularis, the Leopard Toad of southern Africa. Photo by J. Coborn.

animal compositions, which is precisely what makes them so valuable for rearing tadpoles. Pellets are also suitable.

Feeding the froglets only becomes difficult when they have completed metamorphosis and have gone on land. In the wild they find an abundance of small insects and insect larvae, aphids, and young spiders. But who has the time to collect small live food of this kind every day? The city-dweller, at least, is chiefly dependent on food that he can rear himself or store. The rearing of whiteworms and fruitflies is easy. A welcome supplement is young fly larvae. One can sometimes find aphids in fairly large numbers in gardens.

The rearing cages must be furnished in such a way that the froglets or toadlets can quickly and easily catch the food. The food animals must not have the opportunity to hide for any length of time. In the cold season, red midge larvae (bloodworms) are a useful food. It is advisable to offer them individually. Once the frogs and toads have become acclimated to being fed with forceps, feeding is greatly simplified. You then have control of how much the animals eat and which foods they are allowed.

For hygienic reasons, the rearing cage must be furnished in a very uncomplicated way, for

The tiny Oak Toad, Bufo quercicus, *is found in the pinelands of the southern United States. Photo by G. Dingerkus.*

Top: The Marine Toad, Bufo marinus. Photo by M. Gilroy.
Bottom: The Southern Leopard Frog, Rana utricularia. Photo by R. T. Zappalorti.

bark to provide welcome shelter. The bark is also easy to keep moist, but any formation of mildew should be removed immediately. Pieces of ornamental cork are particularly well suited because of their minimal tendency to be attacked by mold. Boil them before use.

For planting, *Tradescantia* is suitable because it is so undemanding. A water level of only a few millimeters is sufficient for it to form a network of roots. The froglets skillfully hunt the food animals on the shoots, which soon form a dense thicket.

you must be able to inspect it regularly and keep it clean. As a substrate, several layers of pieces of peat and rounded-off bricks give the animals the opportunity to retreat from light as needed, while still allowing them to find the food animals that creep around in all of the cracks. Pieces of bark also do good service. For bottom-dwelling froglets or toadlets you can bore holes in these pieces of

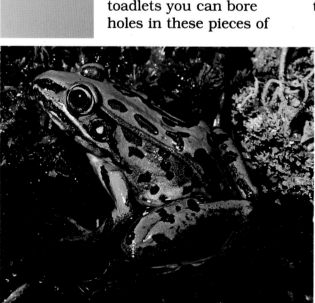

Ample ventilation of the rearing cage must be provided. As far as possible, place it on the balcony but avoid exposure to full sun.

Rearing frogs and toads in this manner is certainly quite laborious, but it is also a source of pleasure and satisfaction for the hobbyist, who will by then already be an advanced terrarium keeper.

The spectacularly colored Dyeing Dart Poison Frog, Dendrobates tinctorius. Photo by R. D. Bartlett.

Lizards

Lizards belong to the reptiles. From the structure of their skin you can deduce that they are capable of tolerating heat and dryness. A thick horny layer protects them against the drying action of the intense and long-lasting solar radiation to which they generally are exposed. The overwhelming majority of lizards literally follow the sun and seek out its warmth, which is a necessity of life for them. Only during the hottest time of day do they avoid the unrelenting scorching rays.

As a rule, their legs are wiry and muscled, and the long tail steers the long agile jumps. In addition, the trunk and tail are often adapted for rapid locomotion. Some lizards are daring climbers; no rocks, no masonry is too steep for them. Some of them, owing to the structure of their feet, are even able to scurry across a ceiling without falling down. There are also lizards with heavy builds, short legs, and short, at times blunt, tails. They move deliberately and the ground is their home. Walls, rocks, bushes, and trees lie outside their domain. In others the evolution to a terrestrial way of life has gone so far that the legs are developed only to a slight extent and the snake-like bodies are capable of wriggling locomotion. There are even lizards that have dispensed with all limbs and wriggle along the ground using only their elongated bodies. Certain species spend the majority of their lives in the ground itself, through which they travel as though swimming.

You must be aware of all this information if you wish to keep reptiles in general and lizards in particular. The furnishing of the cage must be precisely adjusted to their habits. If you do not take this into consideration, keeping the animals will turn into cruelty and the animals will waste away and die. You should always inquire about the provenance of the lizards and also about their size when fully grown. It often happens that inexperienced terrarium keepers are offered young animals that outgrow their cages in a relatively short time.

This large Tegu, *Tupinambis teguixin*, represents a fairly typical lizard, with a forked tongue, distinct head plates, eye lids, and obvious legs. There are many exceptions to this general plan, however. Photo by W. B. Allen, Jr.

LACERTIDS

Strictly speaking, the lacertids (family Lacertidae) are distinguished by a "collar" consisting of fairly large scales on the underside of the neck. Their slender form with the greatly elongated, often very thin tail makes their characteristic lightning-fast movements possible. With the aid of their long,

A pair of Sand Lizards, Lacerta agilis. Photo by B. Kahl.

thin toes they cling fast to rocks. They are also able to make extremely accurate jumps. Their prey, chiefly insects, certainly is also extremely fast and unpredictable in movements. These agile lizards should be given the opportunity to hunt in the terrarium and capture their own food; you should not make obtaining food too easy for them. After all, their often surprising agility is a typical characteristic of these graceful reptiles.

Lacertids are true children of the sun. Their activity is totally dependent on the efficiency of this source of energy. Their maximum diversity, with an almost unbelievable abundance of species, subspecies, and varieties, occurs in southern Europe in the Mediterranean region. The lacertids that live there are significantly more attractively colored and often larger than other

European lizards. Northern lacertids do not do as well in the terrarium as their southern relatives. Their dependence on solar radiation forces us to keep them on a sunny balcony and to construct the cage in such a way that unfiltered sunlight can enter. One is generally compelled to supply supplementary ultraviolet radiation. A buildup of heat must of course be avoided and an ample supply of fresh air is essential for these animals. They are fed with fresh insects and spiders of all kinds and can also temporarily survive on mealworms and even earthworms.

Of the northern green lizards or lacertids, the Sand Lizard *(Lacerta agilis)* is one of the most common. The female exhibits blackish, brown, and whitish eye-spots on a brown or brown-gray background. The males are green on the sides and are especially striking in the spring. A quite attractive variety possesses a broad rust-red dorsal stripe ("erythronota"). The Sand Lizard is not a pronounced climber, and the cage therefore need not be particularly high. A fairly small tree stump serves as a place to sun as well as a hiding place. A stump should not be lacking in any green lizard cage. A lizard that does not go to its hiding place when the sun goes down is probably ill.

The cage is planted with ivy, other climbing plants, a low clump of grass, and

The Viviparous Lizard, Lacerta vivipara, *usually gives birth to living young. Photo by H. Bielfeld.*

Large, active males of the Emerald Lizard, Lacerta viridis, are among the most brightly colored of the lizards. Photo by B. Kahl.

particularly good ventilation cannot be provided. This appears to be one of the most critical problems of all in the keeping of green lizards.

The Viviparous Lizard (*Lacerta vivipara*) generally reaches a length of only 15 centimeters. The rather plain brown animal exhibits, particularly on the sides, flecked markings, but in some specimens the sides appear to be almost uniformly blackish. A pale central longitudinal stripe and one on each side are not always very clearly expressed. The male has an orange and black-flecked belly; the female's is uniformly whitish.

This small lizard likes a certain amount of moisture and also occurs fairly often in moors. A small pile of wood chips and pieces is readily climbed for sunning. The animals can also hide in it. Besides eating insects and spiders, the Viviparous Lizard also accepts earthworms quite readily. This lizard has a pleasant

not too tall but also not too delicate plants such as we find along roads, railway embankments, and other suitable places. A slightly hollowed out stone can serve as a drinking bowl. It is sufficient, however, if the cage is sprayed daily in the morning. The clinging drops of water are licked up by the lizards. The Sand Lizard, up to 20 centimeters in length, as well as the following species, does better in an outdoor terrarium than in an indoor terrarium when

disposition.

The Emerald Lizard *(Lacerta viridis)*, the largest and most beautiful European green lizard, occurs from central and southern Europe to Asia Minor and has a number of different races. In central Europe this true southerner occurs only in very sunny, dry sites and is considerably smaller than in southern Europe, where specimens 40 centimeters and longer are not rare. The conspicuously long tail along with the slender but powerful build betray the nimble runner. The head is robust and the jaws can grab powerfully. The splendid green coloration is interrupted by small black dots in the male and by fairly large black flecks and generally light longitudinal stripes in the female. These sizable lizards should be kept only in very large, airy cages with abundant sunlight and fresh air. In a rocky landscape broken up by only a few robust plants, a fairly large limestone slab is

arranged in such a way that the rays of the sun or a basking lamp strike it vertically. Warmth and irradiation are of prime importance for the well being of these handsome animals.

Correspondingly robust fresh food (grasshoppers, crickets, and the like) must of course be obtained in adequate amounts. Anyone who is not in the position to appropriately meet the needs of these elegant but imposing animals would be better off turning to smaller species, which in elegance and beauty

An Emerald Lizard, Lacerta viridis. *Photo by H. Hansen.*

scarcely fall short of the Emerald Lizard and, in fact, are much more charming.

In a broader sense, the Wall Lizards (*Lacerta [Podarcis] muralis)* are also southerners, and innumerable races and varieties of them have evolved. It really is difficult to say which of them is the most beautiful, such are the unbelievably attractive markings and colors that enrapture us in these unique Mediterranean

The Wall Lizard, Lacerta muralis, *occurs in a bewildering variety of color patterns and subspecies. Today it often is placed in the genus* Podarcis. *Photo by H. Hansen.*

lizards. They are extremely skillful climbers and effortlessly scale with artistic daring the steepest walls and rocks. Their long-clawed toes support them on the slightest roughness or imperfection of the substrate. In addition, they also jump with matchless skill, using the tail as a rudder. If they lose this—and a lizard's tail is easily broken off—then their all-around mobility is

greatly impeded.

The cage for these acrobats of the lizard world must be appropriately constructed. The depth of the terrarium is of secondary importance to the length and, in particular, height. Ample climbing provisions on a sufficiently wide and above all high wall surface must be present. On this rock wall the temperamental life of these animals is played out. Here the males fight for their territories and also hunt flies, butterflies and moths, other insects, and spiders. In this masonry they also seek out their hiding places. If the cage has a sturdy place to stand that is capable of carrying the weight, you can risk building a wall of limestone. Fissures and passages are left as refuges. If the cage cannot be too heavy, then light pumice stone is used to build the wall. The stones are arranged successively in two layers so that a sufficient number of cracks is created.

It is a highly amusing sight when the animals scuffle and chase one another, disappearing into one crack and then appearing in another. If the sun suddenly breaks through on a cloudy day, it will not be long before the slender, handsome animals inquisitively look out from their shelters and then move to their sunning places. The rock wall must of course not be allowed to become too hot. It is also essential to provide for good ventilation of the hiding places. These are built in such a way that water from spraying cannot remain standing in them. Dampness and stuffy air must not be allowed to build up anywhere. Some of the cracks should be planted with robust sun-loving plants. Loamy, firmly pressed in soil anchors and feeds the plants.

If such a cage has a favorable location on a balcony, you will find it difficult to tear yourself away from it. Something is always going on with these lively children of the sun—you cannot take your eyes off their playful frolicking.

Lacerta muralis muralis of central Europe reaches a length of 15 to 18 centimeters and is generally brown, covered with numerous flecks that produce an almost reticulated effect. In the female there is a dark, generally white-bordered, longitudinal band with a row of flecks in the central stripe. The underside may be yellowish white or even red; occasionally it is speckled.

The subspecies *Lacerta muralis brueggemanni,* which occurs principally in northern Italy, displays a beautiful reticulation on the olive-green back.

There are numerous species related to the Wall Lizard in the European countries bordering the Mediterranean that differ from one another in coloration and markings.

Lacerta *(or* Podarcis) lilfordi *is a close relative of the Wall Lizard. Photo by H. Bielfeld.*

Unbelievably large and varied is the selection of these trusting, distinctive creatures that surpass one another in the originality of their coloration and markings. From black, cobalt blue, ultramarine, olive-green, yellow-green, and brown to copper-colored, all nuances are found on the back. Added to this are dark stripes, flecks, dots, and reticulated markings. The colors of the underside range from blue through yellow to red. The wealth of variations goes so far that virtually every isolated rock outcropping, no matter how small, exhibits its own lizard color pattern. From this large assortment only a few that are particularly suited for keeping in the terrarium can be discussed here. Of *Lacerta lilfordi,* whose relatively shorter and thicker tail is conspicuous, there is a unique dark race with a black back and blue underside. There is a race of *Lacerta pityusensis* with a green back and red underside. The races of these two "island lizards" do particularly well in

captivity, although you will always have to count on fights, which occasionally can become serious. Like all of these southern lizards, they have large appetites. In addition to insects of all kinds, they also eat earthworms, slugs, and pieces of meat and fish. They exhibit a particular liking for sweet, overripe fruit, as well as for grapes, raisins, figs,

central stripe. In the southern race the green back is broken up by longitudinal rows of black flecks. Ruins Lizards are larger and more robust than the Wall Lizards. Their heads are also bigger and more powerful. In accordance with their form, they do not produce as graceful and elegant an impression as the Wall Lizards. They are just as

Psammodromus algirus, *the Algerian Sand Lizard of northern Africa and southwestern Europe. Photo by H. Hansen.*

dates, bananas, marmalade, pudding, milk, cream, and the like.

The Ruins Lizard (*Lacerta [Podarcis] sicula*) occurs in the upper half of Italy as *Lacerta sicula campestris* and in the lower part as far as Sicily as *Lacerta sicula sicula.* The green back of the northern race has, in addition to a central stripe of densely packed black flecks, a green longitudinal band on each side of the

highly variable as the other lacertids of the Mediterranean region.

The Algerian Sand Lizard *(Psammodromus algirus)* has completely different habits. It is characterized by large, keeled scales on the upper side that are arranged like roofing tiles. As a ground-dweller, it needs a cage with a large open space. The monotony of the furnishings of rocks and sand is broken up by big

pieces of bark and roots. It likes to burrow in the sand, which it sometimes scatters around the cage. For this reason you should not install the ventilation slit covered with wire mesh too low on the sides. Its range extends from the Iberian Peninsula to southern France and northwestern Africa. It tolerates cool nights but likes the heat of its homeland during the day. Its brown, often bronzy or copper-tinged back, interrupted by two golden yellow longitudinal stripes on each side, is well adapted to the pebbles and low shrubs. Despite its length (20 to more than 25 centimeters) and its robust build, it is

surprisingly fast. Grasshoppers and hard-shelled insects are seized in the powerful jaws. Sand Lizards meet their water requirement by lapping up drops of dew, so you should spray the few robust plants and the rocks with lukewarm water the first thing in the morning.

OTHER LIZARDS

The Slowworm *(Anguis fragilis),* which is found over large areas of Europe and has a range extending into northwestern Africa and Asia, is completely restricted to a terrestrial existence. Its elongated form, its lack of legs, and the resulting wriggling locomotion immediately lead the layman to think of a snake. The rather typical lizard's head with its movable eyelids, however, betrays the fact that it is actually a lizard; in fact, it belongs to the anguids, family Anguidae, along with alligator lizards. The head and tail are not clearly set off from the rest of the body. The relatively long tail, which begins just behind the vent, as in other lizards, breaks off easily and can, if necessary, be cast off voluntarily. The gray or brown scales, because of their shiny smoothness, look like bronze. Some older males also have bluish flecks on the back.

These attractive, lovable animals reach a length of 40 to 50 centimeters. They produce a somewhat awkward impression but manage to wriggle very adeptly through the ground cover. They avoid harsh, hot sunlight and prefer partially shaded, somewhat damp sites with dense ground cover. One finds them after a warm rain on the edges of paths and woodlands. At these times their prey animals, slugs and earthworms, also crawl about. With the aid of their sharp teeth they grab fairly large worms and swallow them with uniform chewing movements.

The Slowworm is for all practical purposes livebearing. The generally gleaming gold juveniles, which in addition to the

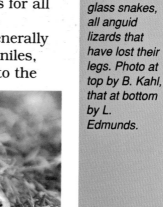

The Sheltopusik, Ophisaurus apodus, *is a close relative of the North American glass snakes, all anguid lizards that have lost their legs. Photo at top by B. Kahl, that at bottom by L. Edmunds.*

black sides also have a dorsal stripe, are even more appealing than the adults. Rearing them is difficult if you try to feed them exclusively on whiteworms, which is a too one-sided diet in the long run. Try to frequently introduce fresh handfuls of moss and balls of leaves from the woods; these have a whole living world of small creatures suitable as food. Although there is

Balkhash and as far south as Iran. The mostly copper-brown upper side exhibits flecking and banding only in young specimens. The lighter underside is brownish to flesh-colored. The bony plates in the skin are even more strongly developed than in the Slowworm and prevent the graceful flexibility of the elongated body that is characteristic of snakes. The Sheltopusik

Scincus scincus, *the Apothecary Skink. Photo by H. Bielfeld.*

also the danger of occasionally introducing pests, this risk is well worth taking because rearing these charming animals really is a fascinating activity.

Related to the Slowworm is the Sheltopusik *(Ophisaurus apodus)*. This powerful, also legless anguid or glass snake is found from the Balkan Peninsula almost as far east as Lake

favors open country with low shrubs and piles of boulders. It attains a length of over 1 meter and hunts fairly large prey animals such as mice and lizards. Snails are apparently its favorite food, and it knows how to crack them open expertly. When snails are not available, you can fool these powerful and strong-biting anguids with empty snail shells containing

chopped lean meat mixed with a pulverized vitamin-calcium preparation. Sheltopusiks also take fairly large grasshoppers and worms. At first quite shy, a lizard will become acclimated with time to its keeper and will take strips of meat from forceps when no live food is available. If two of these voracious anguids have grabbed the same large food animal, then the cylindrical, relatively clumsy lizards rotate like a flash around their own long axis until they have torn the prey apart. Acclimated Sheltopusiks have such large appetites that they even wait for their keeper in order to tear the food from his hand. It therefore does not seem advisable to keep these heavy eaters together with smaller lizards in the same cage. Because they crawl in flat, powerful coils, they need a roomy terrarium with flat stones and a large root as a hiding place. Even robust plants do not survive long in a Sheltopusik cage because the powerful animals soon turn the cage furnishings upside-down.

The skinks are even more adapted to a terrestrial way of life. They need a loose substrate, into which some species burrow completely. In

Top: The shovel-shaped snout of Scincus scincus *is typical of burrowers.* **Bottom:** *An adult Five-lined Skink,* Eumeces fasciatus, *with well-developed head color. Photos by G. Dingerkus.*

open deciduous forests they are usually found in the loose humus layer, in decaying forest mold, and under pieces of bark and stones. The species that occur in the desert burrow like a flash into the loose sand and literally "swim" through it. This manner of locomotion has earned some of them the name "sandfish." The body form is adapted to these highly specialized habits. The skin of these sand-dwelling skinks has a splendid porcelain-like

Calotes calotes *is a common tropical Asian agamid noted for its bright colors. Males often have red heads and are called "bloodsuckers." Photo by J. Bridges.*

glossiness as a result of its smoothness. The head is generally conically pointed in front or is even flattened somewhat like a spatula. The legs are not very long but are robustly built. During the day the use of a heat lamp in the cage is recommended; bottom heating should not be too strong, particularly at night. Skinks, depending on where they are found, chiefly feed on insects of all kinds, their larvae, and spiders. They quickly notice a food animal running over the ground, and you need not wait long for them to appear when food has been introduced. The elegant appearance and, in some cases, the quite attractive coloration make up for the cryptic habits.

In the desert areas of

North Africa lives the 20 centimeters long Apothecary Skink *(Scincus scincus)*. On a yellow or light blue background, wide brown transverse stripes, often with a violet tinge, run across the back. The pointed, tapering head with the overlapping upper jaw is excellently adapted for locomotion in sand. With it this skink burrows in the sand and is able to move through it surprisingly fast.

The Berber Skink *(Eumeces algeriensis)*, which also comes from North Africa, grows to about twice the size of the Apothecary Skink. The orange-red of its flecks and stripes gleams brilliantly. As a substrate for this African skink you should use clean, fine sand in a 12 to 15 centimeters thick layer. A few tough desert plants must be firmly anchored

Uromastyx acanthinurus, the Black Thorny-tailed Agamid. Photo by J. Coborn.

between the rocks, because the bottom will be ploughed up by these animals.

The Five-lined Skink *(Eumeces fasciatus)* comes from the eastern United States. Its length ranges from 14 to 18 centimeters. Juveniles and females have five whitish to yellowish longitudinal stripes on a dark brown, almost black background. These stripes are lacking or reduced in adult males, which in their place exhibit a red tinge on the sides of the head.

Farther to the west in the United States lies the range of the Great Plains Skink *(Eumeces obsoletus)*. Longitudinal rows of fine black or dark brown dots extend over the light gray or yellowish scales. This skink should be given a loose substrate of sand, leaf litter with bark, and isolated flat stones.

Most agamids need fairly large cages. The bodies of these robust and sometimes unbelievably fast lizards are compressed, the head is often broad and short,

and the tail generally is conspicuously long. Some agamids are terrestrial; others can climb and jump very well. The conspicuously powerful hind legs, the pronounced claws, and the long tail facilitate rapid, vigorous locomotion.

The Hardun or Common Agama *(Agama stellio)* inhabits the hot dry regions bordering the eastern Mediterranean Sea. It is not especially colorful, the monotony of the brown back broken only by a few fairly large yellowish and smaller blackish flecks. This almost 30 centimeters desert lizard produces an imposing impression because of its decidedly robust form and virtually "prehistoric" character. This impression is strengthened by the thorny processes on the rear part of the sides of the broad, flat head, on the back, and above all on the tail. Because of its impetuous, shy temperament, it must be carefully acclimated. It is able to hide itself in rock fissures and to climb tree trunks skillfully and unbelievably quickly. The cage should not be lacking piles of rocks and pieces of wood, which offer it

Uromastyx acanthinurus is a plant-eater. It requires a very hot, dry climate to thrive. Photo by H. Bielfeld.

provisions for climbing and hiding. A Hardun will never become finger-tame. With a raised head it spots everything, no matter how carefully you approach the cage. Grasshoppers, large butterflies and moths, and other insects are captured with a firm grip. Like virtually all lizards of the Mediterranean region, the Hardun is also fond of sweet fruit. Because of its timid temperament, this boisterous runner and jumper needs a roomy cage. In the summertime this should, as far as possible, be placed in a sunny but airy location.

Far more attractive and

with a blue tinge. The throat area is yellow, and the underside of the trunk has a yellowish white tint. A "thorny" crest starts at the back of the head on a fold of skin and then extends, although much lower, as far as the tail. The tail is longer than the trunk and helps propel the animal forward when it swims. A large water bowl is indispensable, because this agamid is very fond of water. It also knows how to climb extremely well. It is often found lying asleep on a branch, the thickness of which corresponds to the size of its body.

interesting is the Water Dragon *(Physignathus cocincinus)*, which also exceeds the Hardun in size by a considerable margin. The trunk is more olive-green in color and the tail exhibits distinct transverse banding, while the head is often a handsome green, at times

Sungazers. **Top:** Cordylus giganteus. Photo by K. Lucas, Steinhart Aquarium. **Bottom:** Cordylus cataphractus. Photo by B. E. Baur.

Because of its good jumping ability you should never "make do" with just a climbing tree, but instead should set up at least two of them

so that these beautiful agamids can actually leap from limb to limb and can get enough exercise. At other times they lie on a diagonally rising trunk, the beautiful head raised, and look around. At the necessary temperature of 25 to 30°C (77 to 86°F) they can be quite lively, and you must be quiet, but prepared for anything, when approaching or opening the cage—these lizards are quite shy and often react violently when startled. They then injure their snouts by running into the glass panes, and the injuries heal very slowly if at all. It is advisable with such animals to not only cover the back wall of the terrarium but, as far as possible, also the side walls with rough-barked wood. There the animals can hang on instead of trying to break through the wall. Once they have lost their shyness they provide a great deal of pleasure, for they then become acclimated to the keeper and his handling and even take food from the food stick or forceps. That they can grab and swallow quite respectable bites is not at all surprising. The diet should be varied: fairly large insects (including beetles), meat, fish, frogs, mice, mealworms, bananas, grapes, cherries, and so forth. Even small birds and their eggs as well as small lizards are not rejected. Keeping water dragons is one of the highest points of the terrarium hobby. It requires much effort and demands diligence, patience, and sympathetic understanding. In the care of such animals you must apply all your knowledge and resources. If success is granted, then the satisfaction is immeasurable, for the care of these lizards is not easy.

The Common Sungazer, Cordylus cordylus. Photo by G. Marcuse.

The lizards of the genus *Calotes* from tropical Asia like to drink, but they avoid open water and spend their time in trees and shrubs. The body covering consists of large, keeled scales. Their intimidation behavior is quite pronounced. During territorial fights males display to their rivals by inflating their throat pouch, assuming a "broadside" position to show off the dewlap and crest to greatest effect, and bobbing their heads. Particularly impressive is their ability to change color, which is rarely developed to this degree in other agamid lizards.

The Indian Bloodsucker (*Calotes versicolor*) changes color when "in the mood" or when stimulated. Its head area then turns red (thus the name bloodsucker) and its body turns green, yellow, and black. At other times it exhibits only a brownish olive tint. Once the "contest" has ended, the loser, as a sign of submission, changes to a brownish, even grayish, color. This lizard is very shy at first, and you must slowly acclimate it to yourself and the new environment. It can attain a length of up to 40 centimeters including the tail, and therefore needs a correspondingly large terrarium with sufficient trunks and branches. Robust insects are taken as food. They prefer to drink from dripping water.

The Pinecone Skink of Australia, Trachydosaurus rugosus. Photo by E. Zimmermann.

In the Bornean Bloodsucker (*Calotes cristellatus*) the ability to change color appears to be even more pronounced. It can transform from gray to yellow-brown to a beautiful green with turquoise and reddish flecks, and in extremely rapid order. It reaches an excited state quickly. Handle these interesting, impressive lizards carefully.

The thorny-tailed agamids *(Uromastyx)* resemble to some extent an inexpertly stuffed specimen from an old natural history collection. In some way or other they make an ungainly impression and look as if they come from remote antiquity. The aged looking, relatively small head on the robust, wrinkled, inflatable body, and the spine-armed tail with its whorled, thorny, keeled scales, work together to produce a peculiar impression, primitive and anachronistic. What these animals lack in beauty, in an attractive exterior, is more than made up for by their temperament. They adjust very well to their keeper, soon lose their shyness, take food from the hand, and soon become "house pets." One begins to like these relics from antiquity more and more, finding them not only peculiar but also attractive in their own way, and discovers more and more good qualities in them. During the day they favor a hot basking site like that to which they are accustomed in the dry areas of their homeland. During the night, however, allow the daytime temperature of 25 to 30°C (77 to 86°F) to fall to 15 to 18°C (59 to 65°F). This is particularly true of the African species. The Black Thorny-tailed Agamid *(Uromastyx acanthinurus)* and the Egyptian Thorny-tailed Agamid *(Uromastyx*

The most familiar blue-tongued skink is Tiliqua scincoides. *Photo by E. Zimmermann.*

aegyptius), the latter of which grows to the larger size and can reach a length of over half a meter, come from North Africa. *Uromastyx acanthinurus* is smaller, more widespread, and is more variable in coloration. The Indian Thorny-tail *(Uromastyx hardwickii)* is a more uniform yellowish gray color and may exhibit only a fine dark flecking. Some specimens of *Uromastyx acanthinurus* show a yellowish green or light green back as well as orange-red on the head and black on the legs. Thorny-tails like to burrow and occasionally hide themselves quite deep in the substrate; this is

important to know if you put them in an outdoor terrarium to sunbathe on hot summer days. As juveniles they are supposed to have the sharp teeth typical of the "predaceous" agamids, but later the teeth become adapted to a predominantly vegetable diet. The range of foods eaten is large; yellow dandelion flowers are favored, as are clover and daisies, as well as their leaves. They also accept lettuce, alfalfa, and the like, grated carrot, fruit, pudding, softened maize and rice, and many other things. As with all terrarium animals, continually try new foods. Grasshoppers and other insects should also be offered, since these lizards are not strictly vegetarian.

In the dry steppes and savannahs of Africa are found the strictly terrestrial girdled lizards or sungazers *(Cordylus).* The tail of these lizards is encircled by a whorled arrangement of spiny scales, and the scales of the body, the legs, and, in some species, particularly those of the head are provided with varying numbers of spines that give these animals a

particularly bizarre appearance.

The Giant Sungazer *(Cordylus giganteus)* produces an imposing impression because of its size (over 30 centimeters) and its covering of spines. The large, shingled scales lend the back of the head an especially militant character. This "warrior" often looks around with raised head and grabs everything that it can swallow, including mice. It adjusts very well to its keeper, however. Juveniles are often considerably more attractively colored than adults and sometimes exhibit brown, yellow, and red colors. The bright coloration fades with increasing age.

The Armored Sungazer *(Cordylus cataphractus)* lacks the conspicuous spines on the back of the head but is armed and armored on the upper side, including the legs, with numerous spiny scales stiffened with bone. It does not grow longer than 25 centimeters.

The Common Sungazer *(Cordylus cordylus),* approximately 12 centimeters long, has an

The Common Iguana can be recognized by the enlarged round scale near the angle of the lower jaw and the high, serrated crest. Adults seldom are more than faintly touched with green. Photo by I. Francais.

extensive range in the southern half of Africa. Because of the lack of spines on the back of the head it does not give such a "prehistoric" impression, but it is a particularly appealing terrarium animal. Its small size alone makes it easier to care for. Also attractive is the coloration, which varies depending on origin, from the normal yellow-brown to red-brown and

lizards of the Australian continent, is excellently suited for terraria makes it one of a limited number of highly recommended terrarium animals. It is noteworthy because of its "prehistoric" form and absolutely grotesque exterior. The stout, broad, short tail seems at first glance to differ from the head only in the lack of the broad mouth, the trusting black eyes, the distinct nostrils, and the direction of the large, shiny, mostly black scales. The dark back may be brightened by indistinct light flecks or stripes.

On short, stubby legs, this lizard, which because of its build is almost confined to the ground, moves forward at an easy-going pace, gladly following the warming rays of the sun. In cloudy, cool weather and at night these phlegmatic animals seek out their hiding places in the terrarium. As is true of all ground-dwellers, the cage should have as large a surface area as possible with plenty of room to move around. Clean, fine sand, peat bricks, flat stones, and flat pieces of bark serve as hiding

An Iguana's color reflects his health and mood to a great extent. Photo by I. Francais.

dark-flecked specimens to totally black specimens. They need a great deal of radiant heat when they sun themselves on stone slabs and lie in wait for insects.

The fauna of Australia is rich in peculiarities. Of the Australian reptiles, a curiosity for the terrarium keeper is the Pinecone Skink or Shingleback *(Trachydosaurus rugosus).* The fact that this skink, more than 30 centimeters long, as is true of the majority of other large

places and make up the principal part of the furnishings. A few tough desert plants, firmly anchored in pots, can be installed. A "burrow" filled with dry moss, chunks of peat, and other loose substrate appears to be agreeable to these pronounced ground-dwellers. A shallow water container should be provided. If the walls are at least 30 centimeters high, a cover for preventing escapes is not needed. However, a cage of this kind dries out excessively in the conditions of low humidity present in most homes. You can compensate for this shortcoming by spraying the cage lightly in the morning, but you should avoid striking the animals themselves with water as they appear not to like

this. Keeping these lovable animals outdoors on a balcony in the fresh air and with direct sunshine is quite good for their well-being. A large outdoor cage, specially furnished for this purpose, is a requirement for these basically sluggish children of the sun, one that you should not deny them. As the weather grows colder a "winter rest" of about two months is quite beneficial.

The menu for these delightful, finger-tame

lizards is large and includes a wide assortment of foods: earthworms, slugs, snails, mealworms, other beetle larvae, beetles, grasshoppers, raw liver, meat, fish, white bread soaked in milk, cream, pudding, raw egg yolk, soft-boiled egg, fruit

Swifts are popular lizards and several species are available. The Fence Lizard, Sceloporus undulatus, occurs over much of the United States. Males have bright blue patches on their sides and throat. Photo at top by G. Dingerkus, that at bottom by W. B. Allen, Jr.

juice, sweet fruit, bananas, mushrooms, and other dainties should be offered in rotation. With good individual care the animals become so tame that they run on their own to the plate at dinner time to get their share. This trusting adjustment in the household community makes up for their sluggishness. You will simply no longer wish to do without the Shingleback once it has become acclimated, and you will soon forget the high purchase price.

The Blue-tongued Skink *(Tiliqua scincoides),* which also comes from Australia, reaches a length of over 1 meter and in its form betrays its kinship to the skinks more than the Shingleback does. The tail is longer, the scales are smoother, and the animal is more lively and motile, although certainly not agile. Broad, dark transverse stripes are located on a grayish yellow to reddish brown background. This lizard also eats all sorts of foods and has a pronounced sweet tooth. Do not keep it together with small lizards, because it may show cannibalistic tendencies at any time. When furnishing the terrarium, keep in mind that these skinks may dig and scratch vigorously. With time they become totally confiding, allowing themselves to be taken from the cage and becoming, in a manner of speaking, finger-tame. They may even attempt to get their share at the dinner table. It is no wonder that they enjoy great popularity with terrarium hobbyists.

The old crested male Green Anole at the bottom looks quite different from the normal young adult at the top. Photo at top by M. Gilroy, that at bottom by E. Radford.

IGUANAS AND ANOLES

The iguanids (Iguanidae) are related to the agamids but almost never share the same range with them—iguanids are mostly New World lizards, agamids Old World. They are quite pugnacious, defending their territory with all their energy, and in their behavior often exhibit the same bobbing of the head for intimidating their rivals as do agamids.

The Green or Common Iguana *(Iguana iguana)* is a powerful lizard. Older animals have something "dragon-like" about them. The powerful head with the enlarged scales on the lower jaw and in the throat region and the "pearl" (a gigantic circular scale) under the tympanum give the handsome animal a haughty appearance. The dewlap hangs far downward, with thorny spikes that are far less well developed than those of the jagged crest on the back and tail. In the nape area the crest attains an imposing size and lends a unique impression to these throwbacks to a time when the reptiles ruled the world.

The remarkably intelligent looking eyes, black and surrounded by a narrow yellow and a wide

brown ring, take note of every movement in the room and follow every step of the keeper, whom the iguana learns to recognize. With the powerful claws, which betray its tree-dwelling lifestyle, it scratches on the glass pane of its cage until the door is opened and a treat is offered. Often it does not even wait to be fed, but jumps on the keeper and allows the food to be stuffed into its mouth. It is advisable to put on an old, sturdy jacket, because the uncommonly sharp claws can tear any material. Such a fellow lodger seldom voluntarily returns to its cage. It slowly climbs up and along the furniture, but suddenly

animal must get used to the keeper's hand gradually.

Very young iguanas are charming fellows that are often offered as "babies." Each differs from the other in appearance and temperament. The choice is difficult when you have to select one or two from a group of young animals. Rearing them is not without its problems, and you must occasionally reconcile yourself to a loss. This is all the more sad

A large Knight Anole, Anolis equestris, *has one of the most vicious bites of any common species. Photo by G. Dingerkus.*

decides to take a graceful jump when it has another goal in sight. Never leave it alone in the room even for a moment. If it has spotted something worth striving for, the iguana will stop at nothing to reach it. It is particularly attracted to flowers. Catching and returning it to its cage should take place very quietly and without haste. Above all, during the initial acclimation period you should approach the cage very cautiously. The

because these beautiful, "clever," large lizards become so attached to their keeper and literally become a member of the family. Unfortunately, they grow to a very large size and with time attain a length of 1.5 meters or more. In any case, you should obtain at least two young animals that are already adjusted to each other. The later addition of a strange animal is risky— they do not always stop at head bobbing and spreading of the dewlap.

These handsome iguanas, whose green is only occasionally interrupted by brownish transverse stripes, inhabit the northern part of South America as well as Central America, above all in the vicinity of large rivers. The cage, which should be as large as possible, should contain a water section for the sake of maintaining a high humidity. If you wish to dispense with this, a fine spraying in the morning and in the afternoon as well, if the air is dry, is necessary. A small water bowl will be visited regularly; it should never be without fresh water. A heat lamp provides for the required temperature of 25 to 30°C (77 to 86°F). A robust climbing branch with rough bark will soon be chosen as a resting place. With head pressed to the branch, the lizard lies in the pleasant warmth, the legs held toward the rear or firmly pressed against the trunk. In very roomy cages you can add plants to a section that is not reached by the heat lamp. However, only robust, durable plants that are not eaten by the animals can be used: sanseverias, robust bromeliads, *Monstera deliciosa, Spironaema fragans,* and the like. It is advisable to keep the plants in pots and to change them frequently.

Green Iguanas have definite personalities, and each has its own idiosyncrasies. This is

The Wall Gecko, Tarentola mauritanica. *Photo by J. Coborn.*

apparent mainly during feeding. As large as is the assortment of foods eaten by these animals, they are choosy and unpredictable in food preferences. Scarcely any two specimens will like to eat the same food at the same time. You must recognize this fact if you are to prevent problems, particularly during the colder seasons. Sometimes the problems cannot be solved to the satisfaction of both parties. For this reason you should constantly offer iguanas different foods and should always strive for variety. The most amazing animal and vegetable products are taken by these choosy, primarily vegetarian omnivores: unsprayed lettuce, spinach, dandelion leaves and flowers, chickweed, clover, cauliflower, grapes, sweet cherries, peaches, pears, apples, raspberries, strawberries, melons, pumpkin, rape, carrots, radish and its leaves, lean meat, fish, earthworms, slugs, beetle larvae, mealworms, grasshoppers, newborn mice and rats, and much more. Fairly hard fruits and vegetables should be thinly sliced or grated.

In the summertime you should place the iguana in direct sunshine daily for several hours, but should give it the opportunity to retreat into shade. In the winter the use of a sunlamp twice weekly promotes good health.

The Eastern Fence Lizard *(Sceloporus undulatus)* belongs to the genus of spiny lizards *(Sceloporus)* and comes from the drier regions of the eastern and central United States. It prefers sandy coniferous forests, where it likes to sun itself on fences, wood piles, and tree stumps, and while doing so often assumes a lighter coloration. In keeping with its habitat, it is brown to blackish above, but the males possess large iridescent blue patches under the throat and on the sides of the belly. The short head with the blunt snout bobs vigorously when the lizard displays. The coarsely keeled and spiny scales overlap like shingles; on the tail they take on a thorny character. This extraordinarily amusing lizard is some 20 centimeters long. It eagerly seizes and shakes its prey, which consists of spiders and insects. If you provide ample sun and warmth, it makes a lovable, amusing terrarium animal.

The forest iguanas *(Polychrus marmoratus* and *Polychrus acutirostris)* from South America are excellently camouflaged by their form and changeable coloration. They are about 40 centimeters long, with the tail accounting for about two-thirds of the total length. The tails are used for maintaining balance when they hang from a branch by their long, powerful hind legs before a jump, from which they then shoot like an arrow from a crossbow. Provide plenty of jumping branches as well as smaller branches for these arboreal, relatively long-legged iguanids. Quietly but extremely adeptly, they climb around in the branches like chameleons, grasping the twigs with their specialized grasping feet (the inner toes pointed to the inside, the outer toes toward the outside). They are generally greenish in color, often with suggestions of transverse stripes on the sides and black lines around the eye area. They have the ability to change their color. They skillfully stalk their prey, which

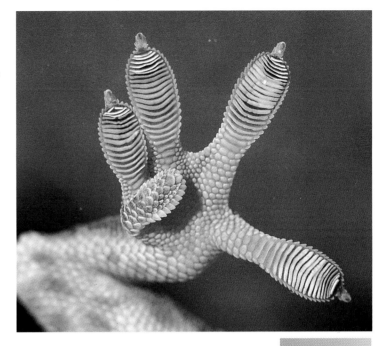

primarily consists of insects. Despite their quiet habits, give them a fairly large cage in order to be able to install sufficient climbing branches.

In the southeastern United States the Green Anole (*Anolis carolinensis*)

The Tokay Gecko, Gekko gecko, *is one of the most commonly kept geckos. It is one of the few lizards with a strong and distinct voice. Photos by K. T. Nemuras.*

lives on trees, shrubs, and fences in not too wet regions. It is often recommended for inclusion in the tropical rain-forest terrarium, but actually it favors only slightly damp localities in regions of relatively dry character. Its ability to change color extremely rapidly has also given it the misleading name "American chameleon." In only a few minutes the beautiful emerald-green upper side can change to a cocoa-brown. This process is all the more remarkable because it does not take place uniformly, so that for a short time the animal is often flecked with both green and brown. The coloration at any particular time of these attractive and peculiar arboreal lizards is dependent upon temperature, light, and, above all, state of excitement.

The pronounced territorial instincts become apparent through the impressive threat behavior of the male. Accompanied by vigorous head bobbing, the large, otherwise barely visible throat fan is spread, displaying its wine-red color. The entire body is raised and is enlarged as a result of flattening of the sides. When the large, deeply indented mouth is also opened threateningly, the most extreme possible intimidation posture is complete. The small throat fan of the female can only be spread slightly.

The toes are an adaptation to an arboreal way of life; they are enlarged toward the tips and are equipped with pads covered with fine hair-like scales on the underside. These rows of "adhesive" scales additionally are provided with the tiniest of hooklets, which enable the agile animals to cling to the irregularities of virtually any surface. With them the anole can gain a footing even on smooth branches and the glass walls of the terrarium. Additionally, each toe also has a long, sharp claw. Rotating around their long axis with unbelievable agility, these trapeze artists of the lizard world can jump from, for example, a seemingly hopeless starting position from the side wall of the terrarium to a vertical branch.

All of their movements are elegant and charming. They are grace personified. If you examine the head and trunk separately, however, then a curious contradiction becomes apparent: the broad head

Leopard Geckos, Eublepharis macularius, are now being bred in captivity on a regular basis and make excellent pets. Large specimens enjoy an occasional pink mouse. Photo by B. Kahl.

sits on a long, slender, elegant trunk. All together, however, the effect is harmonious. In a downright "coquettish manner" the head is turned diagonally from time to time in order to eye the observer.

Install numerous branches in an airy cage for these lizards. Appropriate climbing plants include *Hoya carnosa* and *Scindapsus.* These appealing animals often hang head-down from a climbing plant when sleeping and are then so superbly camouflaged that you must search a long time to find them. For the most part, individual specimens have their fixed, customary sleeping places.

A tall, well-planted terrarium with these dainty lizards, which nevertheless can be so pugnacious, is one of the most beautiful sights to be found in the terrarium hobby. Owing to the lightness and agility of the 15 to 18 centimeters anole, it is possible to plant fairly small, bright-blossomed bromeliads on the branches and truly assemble a luxuriant "slice of nature." Dripping moisture must be avoided, and it really is not required by the bromeliads. Spraying the cage once or twice a day is sufficient. The lizards like to quench their thirst by licking up the drops.

Anoles eat a large assortment of foods. Virtually anything that is found in a bush is eaten: flies, grasshoppers, butterflies and moths, spiders, and much else besides. The sun-loving Green Anoles show off their complete character especially when they are hunting lively flying insects. They literally race after butterflies and complete the most daring jumps to reach the prey. Naturally the full activity is only achieved at the necessary temperature. During the day the temperature should be 25°C (77°F) or higher, and good ventilation must be provided. At night a temperature of 18 to 22°C (65 to 72°F) is sufficient. In the wintertime the animals can get by with less warmth. The activity and appetite decrease considerably, however, at a temperature of 15 to 18°C (59 to 65°F). This winter rest period may be extended to two to three months only with well-fed animals.

The Knight Anole (*Anolis equestris*), which comes from Cuba, can attain a length of more than 40 centimeters and is one of the largest species of anole, although it should be remembered that the tail is about twice as long as the head and trunk. This species of course requires correspondingly sturdy furnishings with firmly anchored climbing branches. The food should also be robust and voluminous.

GECKOS

The geckos are characterized by several anatomical and biological peculiarities that distinguish them from other lizards. The various species differ from one another in the sounds they produce and in the structure of their toes. The structure of the pupil also varies in different species. The majority of geckos do not have the movable eyelids characteristic of other lizards; instead, the eyelids are fused together into a transparent plate (the spectacle or brille) as in the snakes. In these geckos the eye therefore cannot be cleaned by the blinking of the eyelid; instead, the long tongue is used to lick the brille. Most geckos are crepuscular or nocturnal animals and possess vertical pupils, but the diurnal geckos are characterized by round darker. The back has rough tubercular scales that are usually arranged in rows. These provide excellent camouflage for these always very shy animals. Only two toes are equipped with claws, but all of the lobes are, as in the anoles, covered with the tiniest hooked bristles.

A hatchling Phelsuma *with its virtually inflexible egg. Photo by R. G. Sprackland.*

pupils. The typical gecko's body is moderately to strongly flattened. The short neck generally carries a blunt, wide, flat head that is somewhat unusual for a lizard. The tail may be very brittle.

The Wall Gecko (*Tarentola mauritanica*) inhabits the countries bordering the western Mediterranean Sea. They are usually yellow-brown above but can become significantly paler or

The pressing of the undersides of the toes to the substrate makes possible such a firm hold that these generally 12 to 15 centimeters lizards seem able to defy the laws of gravity. It is incredible how they can run around upside-down on even the glass cover plate of the terrarium as they stalk food or scuffle with one another.

Although they are crepuscular animals, they

like to expose themselves to evening and morning sun. Agile and nimble, they also flit about the house walls by day. They avoid the midday sun, however. The dry cage should be sprayed before the animals have left their hiding places. These are best installed in the rear wall of the cage. The rear

Phelsuma standingi, one of the many day geckos that have recently entered the market. Photo by K. T. Nemuras.

wall must be so tight-fitting that the agile animals cannot force themselves behind it. Once they do this they are very difficult to remove. All hiding places should be easily accessible to the keeper. Water should never be allowed to collect, because these lizards, which definitely favor dry conditions, are quite afraid of water. They find even

spraying unpleasant. At a temperature of 25°C (77°F) or higher you can derive much enjoyment from the antics of these agile creatures. They will never become confiding, however, and are best observed from some distance away or toward evening under red light. They skillfully capture flies, grasshoppers, and spiders, and in twilight also cockroaches and crickets.

The Tokay Gecko *(Gekko gecko)*, from Southeast Asia, is a robust lizard reaching a length of up to 35 centimeters. The strength and pugnacity of this lizard are just as impressive as its size. At a temperature of 30°C (86°F) or higher this nocturnal predator shows that, despite its quiet temperament, it is definitely not lacking in spirit. Males, in particular, are quite pugnacious toward one another. When irritated, the Tokay threatens by opening its mouth wide and making quacking noises. Cockroaches, crickets, fairly large grasshoppers, and even other lizards and newborn mice are

effortlessly overpowered by this voracious eater. It eventually becomes acclimated to its keeper, overcoming its initial shyness and taking food from forceps. This method of feeding is particularly useful when presenting fugitive, secretive food animals like cockroaches and crickets. Drinking water is licked up in drop form. You should not, however, spray the animals themselves— the Tokay avoids water and can literally be thrown into a frenzy if you spray it. After a meal it wipes off its mouth with its tongue with the contentment of a satisfied gourmet.

The monotony of the light gray ground color of the back is broken by small bluish and reddish spots. The coloring of this species is thus more pleasing and lively than that of most of its nocturnal cousins. The vertical pupil in the yellowish eye betrays the nocturnal habits of this follower of civilization, which appears to prefer to establish its territory in human dwellings. In this species the clinging ability characteristic of most geckos is developed to an astounding degree. These powerful creatures can stalk an insect with amazing agility on the underside of the terrarium cover before seizing it in a flash in their powerful jaws without relinquishing their upside-down position. This peculiar lizard is an attractive, interesting and virtually ideal terrarium animal, especially for those who can devote time to their animals only toward evening.

Although the Asian Leopard Gecko *(Eublepharis macularius)* is, at a length of 30 centimeters, not much smaller than the Tokay, it in no way produces a robust impression. In

The most commonly seen day gecko is Phelsuma madagascari-ensis, also one of the most attractive species. Photo by W. B. Allen, Jr.

contrast to the relatively large head, the legs are long and thin. The toes do not possess any clinging lamellae, but do have claws. These long-legged nocturnal geckos run around on the ground, where they also have their hiding places. These geckos possess true eyelids. Their markings and colorations are attractive. Juveniles exhibit a distinct series of broad black-brown transverse bands on a light background, but older specimens have characteristic dense, prominent, black-brown spots and flecks on a yellow-brown background that give the animal its common name. In old animals weakly suggested

insects, spiders, and the like. Once acclimated, they even take pieces of meat (fortified with calcium and vitamins) from the feeding stick.

The oddness of the geckos, their biological peculiarities, and their fascinating behavior are combined with the charm and beauty of the sun-loving day geckos of Madagascar *(Phelsuma)*. That they are expensive and difficult to find should not deter anyone truly determined to keep them. Recently several species have been bred in good numbers for the hobby.

These lively, extremely agile geckos are most active during the day, especially in the afternoon. Males are incompatible with one another and strenuously defend their territories, so serious fights can occur. Warmth, sun, and a certain amount of humidity soon make these geckos feel right at home in a tall terrarium generously provided with plants and branches. Always provide good ventilation. At first very shy, the majority of these lovable creatures soon become accustomed to the

Phelsuma cepediana, one of the more brightly patterned day geckos. Photo by G. Marcuse.

transverse stripes may be visible on the body. These terrestrial geckos do quite well in captivity and eat

keeper and take insects and spiders from his forceps. They also like to eat sweet, overripe fruit, such as banana mash, and like to lick honey from a hanging walnut shell. In a separate walnut shell offer these lizards (and other geckos) small pieces of calcium blocks. They like to drink and drink often, licking up drops of water with their tongues from the leaves of climbing plants and bromeliads.

The smaller species, which barely grow larger than 10 centimeters long, are exceedingly delightful creatures and are particularly well suited for medium-sized cages thickly planted with tropical plants. When these jewels of the reptile world flit about on blooming epiphytes, it is a sight to behold for even the most demanding of terrarium hobbyists.

The Madagascar Day Gecko *(Phelsuma madagascariensis)* is almost twice as large as the following smaller

species, and at a size of over 20 centimeters it is not only longer than them, but in general is also more robust. It thus can easily handle fairly large food animals (grasshoppers, crickets, smooth caterpillars, and the like). It likes to sit on thick trunks, around which it edges when danger threatens. For this species the hiding places should not be located on the rear wall, because it then generally remains quite shy for a long time. It meets its drinking requirements by licking up drops of water. If you mist the bromeliads it will sometimes lick its own face and eyes as well as the wet leaves. In small bowls or walnut shells it should always have supplies of water, calcium, honey, and vitamins. The terrarium, which should be as roomy as possible, should be located in a

The Gold-dust Day Gecko, Phelsuma laticauda, is a relatively recent import and certainly one of the most attractive of an exceptionally pretty group of species. Photo by K. T. Nemuras.

quiet area of the house. These beautiful animals, which are popular because of their green ground color with red flecking, are always on the watch and observe everything that takes place in their vicinity. The eggs are affixed to surfaces here and there by the female; usually two are attached together. These handsome lizards feel most comfortable at a temperature of 25 to 28°C (77 to 82°F). Keep them in pairs in roomy terraria. The males call loudly, producing a sound like the clucking of a hen, only softer.

The Striped Day Gecko *(Phelsuma lineata)* is characterized by a whitish longitudinal band on each side. Large, irregular red flecking stands out against the handsome green of the back.

The Gold-dust Day Gecko *(Phelsuma laticauda)* is also characterized by bright red flecking on a green background. The nape and anterior back seem to be powdered with gold dust as a result of the finest yellow-gold mottling. The large dark eyes with round pupils typical of diurnal geckos are surrounded by light blue in this particularly attractive species, and even the tail exhibits a blue shimmer. Without doubt the Gold-dust Day Gecko is the most beautiful of all *Phelsumas,* even if the relatively broad, flattened tail cannot compete with the elegant form of the other species.

CHAMELEONS

The chameleons (family Chamaeleonidae) produce the oddest impression in regard to form and habits. The sharply compressed body supports a large head that is often provided with ridges, tubercules, folds, and even horns. In healthy specimens the conically protruding eyes, the eyelids of which are almost totally fused to leave a relatively small pupil opening, can be rotated in all directions independently of each other. Thus a chameleon is able to watch a food animal with one eye while the other is keeping tabs on the keeper. When both eyes are brought into focus on the prey, the mouth slowly opens and the incredibly long tongue darts out and seizes the prey. The tongue with the prey is then withdrawn more slowly into the mouth, where the prey is crushed noisily and swallowed. Chameleons are typical "prey ambushers," often waiting

The Common Chameleon, Chamaeleo chameleon, *is the only chameleon that ranges north into Europe. Photo by H. Zimmermann.*

quietly for long periods. Give them ample climbing branches, the diameters of which correspond to the size of their grasping feet. The feet have evolved into pincers, so on the front feet the inner three and the outer two, and on the hind feet the inner two and the outer three, fingers or toes have fused together into a "vise." The prehensile tail is often rolled up when in resting position.

Highly developed and nothing less than unbelievable is the well-known ability to change colors, which is triggered by moods, external stimulation, and light and temperature effects. To a certain extent you can determine the well-being of a chameleon by its color. Chameleons can in the truest sense of the words "blacken with rage." They are loners, so you should allow for this and keep them, at most, in pairs.

The animals are also disturbed by the addition of too many food insects (above all grasshoppers, caterpillars, and flies). Drops of water are "shot down" with the tongue. In good weather it does the chameleons obvious good when they are placed in an outdoor terrarium in a tall bush. If you hang fly-attracting bait inside the cage (meat and the like), the chameleons simultaneously have fresh air, sunshine, and food—and they are "kept busy." Their care is not easy; suitable food must be procured constantly. Mealworms are at best suitable as a very temporary emergency measure.

The Common Chameleon *(Chamaeleo chamaeleon)* attains a length of 25 centimeters or more and inhabits the lands bordering the Mediterranean Sea on the eastern, southern, and

reaches a length of about 25 to 30 centimeters. Only slightly larger is Jackson's Chameleon *(Chamaeleo jacksoni)* from East Africa. It generally exhibits a dark green, brown-flecked coloration. With its three head horns, the male produces an imposing impression.

Top: Jackson's Chameleon, Chamaeleo jacksoni. Photo by W. Kastle. **Bottom:** The Flap-neck Chameleon, C. dilepis. Photo by J. Bridges.

western sides, although it is now found only rarely in southern Spain. It is basically olive-green in color. The occiput carries only suggestions of lobes. These lobes are more clearly expressed in the Flap-neck Chameleon *(Chamaeleo dilepis)*, which occurs in the southern half of Africa. Its ground color is green, and it

The optimal temperature for chameleons varies depending on where they come from; it should be about 22 to 28°C (72 to 82°F) during the day and somewhat lower at night, depending on the animal's provenance. Before purchasing such a valuable and unfortunately delicate animal you should study the specialist literature. Chameleons are widely sold and often fall into the wrong hands.

Crocodilians

Crocodilians have had bad reputations since antiquity because of their voraciousness and dangerousness. Even today, writers of travel books and news stories are still obsessed with this "leviathan" of the Bible. These accounts are not always exaggerated, because some species can be truly dangerous when fully grown. In their behavior, the individual species and to a certain extent the individuals of a species as well are quite variable.

Only very young specimens of a few species are suitable for keeping in the aqua-terrarium. These babies can be remarkably lovable creatures. These eventual "monsters" have a pronounced "baby face" in their first year of life, and they produce an unusually comical effect with their initial awkwardness and the early childhood proportions. Their attachment to their keeper and the fact that they definitely "know" him and are able to distinguish him from other people immediately allows them to win over quickly even those persons who are not yet familiar with these larger reptiles. Unfortunately, with time they can attain a size that

This young Nile Crocodile, Crocodylus niloticus, *was hatched on a crocodile farm in South Africa. Photo by G. Dingerkus.*

The bellow of a large American Alligator, Alligator mississippiensis, can be heard for literally miles. No crocodilian makes a suitable household pet.

simply prohibits keeping them in the home. Therefore, before the purchase of a crocodilian you must decide in whose hands you will later be able to place it with a clear conscience.

The external appearance of the crocodilians is familiar. The bone-reinforced scales are characteristic. The scales are raised into a saw-like crest on the tail. Webs between the toes point to the aquatic habits. These aquatic reptiles swim rapidly and silently by wriggling their powerful tails. The snout of the flat, powerful head is relatively elongated. The large mouth is armed with sharp teeth that are continually replaced. At the back of the mouth, the esophagus can be closed by means of a tightly fitting flap, so that even when the crocodilian is under water with a closed mouth, atmospheric air reaches the lungs unimpeded through the nostrils. Sometimes only the elevated nostrils as well as the projecting eyes protrude above the water's surface. The nostrils are tightly closed when the animal is under water.

Crocodilians prefer to stay in the water and will return to it at any sign of danger. The animals like to lie relaxed in the water, the head supported on a warm stone. Any prey that is captured on land is pulled back into the water, where it is swallowed. The aquarium must have a heatable land section. It can be built from gutter tiles containing an aquarium heater. The heater is firmly anchored so that it cannot be smashed to pieces by these reptiles, which are very violent when feeding.

The water section must be large enough that the animals can move freely in it. The depth of the water should permit the head to stick out. The land section is heated from above with a heat lamp. Warmth is a requirement for these reptiles from hot climates. A wide drainage pipe simplifies the frequent cleaning of the cage and the indispensable water changes that must be carried out at one- to two-day intervals.

The food (small fishes, narrow strips of lean meat, or fish cut to size) is offered with long wooden forceps. The animals are generally very excited and reckless at feeding time. You should therefore exercise caution to make sure that an animal does not injure itself or accidentally grab your hand in the process. They wait intently for feeding time. At other times as well they observe every movement in the room and react promptly to the accustomed keeper. They display their virtually insatiable appetite and other typical behavior only at temperatures of about 25°C (77°F) or more. In the summertime you should at least occasionally place them in direct sunshine, and good ventilation of the cage of course must be provided. Hot, stuffy air can kill a crocodile.

The American Alligator *(Alligator mississippiensis)* can potentially reach a length of 4 to 5 meters when fully grown. The head is somewhat slimmer than that of the caimans, from which the alligator also differs by the absence of the "spectacles," the bony ridge between the eyes. The fourth tooth of the lower jaw is not visible from outside when the mouth is closed (visible in the true crocodiles). Very young specimens up to a length of about 30 centimeters are exceptionally amusing little creatures, and look quite attractive with their yellow vertical bands on a black background. When they swim up, quacking and growling with raised head to beg for food, at the same time wagging the head and tail back and

American Alligators only a few feet long retain parts of the yellow juvenile pattern, especially on the tail. Photo by G. Dingerkus.

These baby Alligator mississippiensis represent some of a brood of 3-month-old American Alligators that carry a gene for a type of albinism. Photo by E. Radford.

forth in excitement, one is reminded of a young, clumsy puppy. They become quite tame and make a good-natured impression as long as they are still this young. Later, of course, you must be cautious when dealing with them. This alligator, which lives in the southeastern United States, does not necessarily require the same high temperatures as most other crocodilians.

America is divided in two by the Equator, and it is now established in the wild and reproducing in a few southern states of the United States. It has also been bred on alligator farms. In juveniles, dark brown to blackish flecks and stripes decorate an olive-colored background. The distinguishing mark of the Spectacled Caiman is the curved bony ridge on the upper snout connecting the front corners of the eyes. In general, it does not become as confiding as the American Alligator and is more likely to attack its keeper. It reaches a length of only 2 to 2.5 meters. This

At night, in particular, the temperature can be allowed to fall to about 20°C (68°F) without harm.

More fastidious in this respect is the Common Caiman *(Caiman crocodilus)*, which includes the form commonly called the Spectacled Caiman. Its range in Central America and the northern and central parts of South

is the form usually available in pet shops.

A baby caiman really does look delightful with its rounded belly, thin neck, thin little legs, the childish head with its duck bill, and the large eyes with the vertical pupils. When it comes waddling up begging for food and opens its mouth, armed with teeth, before greedily grabbing a fish, you can get some idea of what the little fellow will one day become. Once caimans have grabbed the prey, under no circumstances do they give it up voluntarily. Eagerly, almost in a frenzy, they shake the head back and forth, lift it steeply, and pleasure. Almost imperceptibly you will grow fond of the comical, amazingly active creatures that are remarkably "intelligent" for reptiles.

Crocodilians are now protected by much legislation and are seldom available. The tremendous vitamin, calcium, and

submerge it again under water, trying to find some way to manage a piece that is too large. Only after a long time, when the large bite does not pass down the throat, is it discarded and then ignored. It is better to give such juveniles only narrow, longish pieces that they can swallow without difficulty. The feeding of these imps is truly a sunlight demands of young caimans make them unsuitable as pets for any but the most experienced hobbyists. Few survive more than a few months in the hands of an inexperienced terrarium keeper.

Baby Spectacled Caimans, Caiman crocodilus, have a "cute" baby-face and awkward motions for the first year or so. Photo by A. Norman.

Turtles

Turtles have a unique adaptation of their body structure that sets them apart from all other reptiles: a shell incorporating the ribs. Parts of the skeleton have been joined with components of the skin to form bony plates, and these in turn have been fused together into a single protective shell that is generally covered with horny plates. It encloses the body and, when danger threatens, in most species it also allows the head and legs to be drawn in for protection. The ventral component of the shell, the plastron, is always flattened or slightly concave. The dorsal armor, the carapace, usually is well-arched in the tortoises but in the aquatic turtles is less strongly arched and often almost flat.

Of the tortoises, the Greek Tortoise *(Testudo hermanni)* is sometimes available. If possible, keep it in the outdoor terrarium or on the balcony as long as weather permits. Room air is too dry for it in the long run. During cool weather keep it in a large terrarium with air that is not too dry and do not allow it to roam around the room the whole day. Juveniles, in particular, are appealing creatures. They become accustomed to their keeper and take food from his hand, especially when it is a special treat. They are primarily vegetarians. A rotating menu of lettuce, cabbage, dandelion, clover, tomatoes, and sweet fruit should be offered. Chopped lean beef to which a small amount of calcium supplement powder has been added is also eaten readily and should be offered regularly. They drink clear, not too cold water. About once a week place the tortoise in a lukewarm bath for about half an hour. The water should be deep enough so that the tortoise can just barely stick its head comfortably out of the water.

If you notice that the animals are restless in the fall and seem to want to dig themselves in, they may be ready for over-wintering. About one week after the last feeding and one to two days after the last especially prolonged bath, place them for over-wintering in a sturdy box with moss, leaves, and

loose forest soil mixed with coarse chunks of peat. The box is sprinkled with just enough water to keep it from not drying out completely. Above all, the air in the over-wintering room should not be too dry. The box is covered over and closed with wire mesh so that no rats, mice, or cats can get in (even by chewing the sides). You should not, however, force over-wintering, and for small animals and most indoor

pets over-wintering may be a dangerous idea.

Distinguishing *Testudo hermanni* from *T. graeca* are the double carapace scute above the base of the tail (the supracaudal), the horny nail at the tip of the tail, and the lack of pointed spurs on the thighs. The Moorish Tortoise *(Testudo graeca)* possesses an undivided (single) supracaudal scute above the tail and has no horny terminal nail, but it does have a conical horny

The Greek Tortoise, Testudo hermanni, should not be confused with the Moorish Tortoise (T. graeca) because of the mismatched scientific and common names. This nice T. hermanni is from southern Europe. Photo by A. Jesse.

The Moorish Tortoise, Testudo graeca, once was imported in large numbers from northern Africa. Today Testudo is hard to find on the American market and is (or will soon be) banned from the market in several European countries. Photo by B. Kahl.

scale or spur on the inside of the thighs on either side of the base of the tail. Its range extends from southeastern Europe through North Africa and Asia Minor as far as Iran. Specimens from North Africa once were frequently imported. Because of its misleading scientific name, this species was formerly called the Greek Tortoise; it does not occur in Greece. They require more warmth and are more sensitive to cold than is *Testudo hermanni,* which occurs only in southern Europe.

The European Pond Turtle *(Emys orbicularis)* has amphibious habits.

With a certain degree of streamlining, the almost flat carapace is adapted to the aquatic way of life. The yellowish streaks on the generally blackish carapace are more or less clearly expressed in typical specimens. The same is true of the very attractive yellow-spotted head markings in some specimens. The broad hind feet with strong webbing between the toes are good indicators of an actively swimming, very agile species. They like to climb up on tree trunks or rocks above the water in order to sun themselves. When danger threatens, however, they drop in a flash into underwater plant thickets.

Keep these turtles in an aqua-terrarium. For the land section use a few well-rounded stones, certainly never rough ones. More suitable is a section of cork bark that can be fixed between the front and rear panes of an aquarium. A basking lamp produces the necessary warmth above the land section. The water depth should be somewhat greater than the width of the carapace so that the animals can turn under water at any time if they happen to get themselves into an upside-down position. Like many other aquatic turtles, this species often sheds shell scutes. In healthy turtles this is a natural process much like a snake shedding its skin.

Aquatic turtles are chiefly carnivorous. Fish is absolutely to be preferred to mammal flesh. Small balls can be kneaded from very lean chopped beef mixed with calcium powder, but only as an emergency food until something better is available. Ground shrimp shells can also be used to meet the necessary calcium requirement. The shells are softened before feeding and are cleaned of unusable particles.

Large aquatic turtles require large quarters and heavy filtration; most would do best in a garden pool. Here two South American sidenecks, Phrynops gibbus, *flank a European Pond Turtle,* Emys orbicularis. *Photo by M. Gilroy.*

Earthworms should also be offered from time to time. Vegetable matter (lettuce, other greens) should be offered, even if they are often rejected.

Because of their lively, appealing temperaments as well as their striking, bright markings and coloration, very young North American slider turtles (especially the Red-eared Slider, *Pseudemys scripta elegans)* and allies have often been kept as pets. Although the temperature may temporarily be allowed to fall substantially in wintertime, they only display their lively natures at temperatures of 25°C (77°F) or more. The aquarium heater that is used to heat the water is for safety's sake concealed in a roofing tile. A basking lamp should be installed about 25 to 30 centimeters above a decorative cork bridge so that the horny scutes of the carapace do not dry out and fall off prematurely because of too much heat.

A young Painted Turtle, Chrysemys picta. Paints make excellent, adaptable pets. Photo by R. D. Bartlett.

It is an amusing and delightful sight when the baby sliders, whose carapaces often are no more than 4 centimeters long, pile up under the heat lamp, each trying to get the best spot. With comical contortions they attempt to stretch their broad, paddle-like legs toward the warming rays. Regular direct exposure to sunlight is very good for their health. These youngsters should also be offered abundant amounts of freshly caught aquatic insects or their larvae, daphnia, and aquatic snails, as well as lettuce and other greens. Heavy supplements of calcium and vitamins are essential to prevent rickets and soft-shell.

Of the various sliders and allies that become available, the False Map Turtle *(Graptemys pseudogeographica)* is particularly well suited for

keeping in the turtle aquarium because it attains a length of only 12 to 22 centimeters. The serrated central keel of the brown-black carapace is conspicuous, and the plastron and carapace are often intricately patterned in yellow. Most striking of all are the yellow stripes on the shiny black head, the yellow stripes on the neck and legs, and the yellow-bordered eye.

There are numerous other turtles and tortoises that are suitable for keeping in the terrarium or aqua-terrarium. Single specimens are occasionally available through pet shops, though the cost often is high. Remember that turtles need warmth, cleanliness, a varied diet, good basking facilities, and lots of vitamins and minerals (especially calcium) added to the diet.

Snakes

Snakes have been objects of superstitious notions since ancient times. The silent gliding; the "snaking" of the elongated, legless body; the "glassy stares"; and the venomousness of certain species all have contributed to the fact that the vast majority of people are completely opposed to snakes. But some snakes make very attractive, elegant, and interesting terrarium animals. Many of them are extraordinarily retiring and, at least during the initial period spent in captivity, extremely shy. We find no sign of "malicious cunning" or "treacherous guile." One needs great patience and sympathetic understanding when caring for snakes. With time even these "outlaws" become accustomed to their keeper, and the reciprocal relationship will certainly be a trusting one.

When dealing with snakes, quiet, well-measured movements are required. Haste, nervousness, and impatience must be avoided. Usually the keeper himself is to blame if he happens to be bitten. Many snakes defend themselves less by biting than by discharging their smelly droppings when held in the keeper's hand. It is particularly important to leave snakes alone when they are about to molt. The animals are quite helpless before this occurs and produce a decidedly dull, unwell impression when in this condition. Because the entire skin, including that over the eyes, is replaced at one time, snakes are virtually blind in the several days before molting (when you can see the characteristic "blue eye"). This uncertainty causes them to be aggressive when they suspect a threat. They need warmth and an adequate bath to be able to molt properly. The old skin is first rubbed off in the snout area before being shed in one piece. For this purpose the animals need rough branches with "tight spots" that make shedding the skin easier as they slip through them. Like the phoenix risen from the ashes, they appear as if newly created, gleaming with fresh, bright colors after shedding the old dull skin. A magnificent sight! Feed them soon after molting, for their spirits seem to be reawakened after the apparently quite difficult molting process. It is a pleasure to observe the beautiful, elegant, lithe animals in this "rejuvenated" state.

Snakes like to defecate in their bath. In addition of snakes is almost certainly caused by an infection brought about by unsanitary conditions.

All of the furnishings of the cage should be as well secured as possible. If a newly acquired snake has been introduced into a

to the droppings, you often find yellowish white calcareous masses that are a form of urine. An immediate water change must be carried out, for the snakes of course also drink from this water. They are extraordinarily clean and are very sensitive to any sort of soiling of the cage and water. Serious stomatitis terrarium or if the terrarium has been newly refurnished, the snake will range restlessly through every corner. Everything will be tested with the tongue. No corner will go unnoticed, and no opportunity to escape will be missed. After a while the animal will calm down and find a favorite spot where it will spend most of

A red-phase Mangrove Salt Marsh Snake, Nerodia clarkii compressicauda, from Florida. Photo by W. B. Allen, Jr.

its time. Only occasionally are snakes seized by an inexplicable restlessness, by something like a "migratory instinct." For days on end they will then wander through the cage and search for a way to escape. During this restless period you should not keep them at too warm a temperature and should offer food repeatedly, but otherwise disturb them as little as possible. This restlessness often occurs in the summertime and is sometimes associated with an interruption in feeding.

Snakes are widely distributed throughout the world. There are some 3000 species and many subspecies. These for the most part are completely harmless and lively, even almost hasty in their little movements. It is not easy to hold them. The majority of snakes are colubrids that can be recognized by their long, conspicuously slender body that gradually tapers to a slender, pointed tail.

The most familiar snakes perhaps are the water snakes *(Natrix, Nerodia,* etc.). Keep them in a terrarium that is as roomy as possible and has a sufficiently large water section. This should be strictly separated from the land section, the water never being allowed to

The Viperine Water Snake, Natrix maura, is one of the more popular aquatic snakes on the European market but it is virtually unavailable in America. Photo by B. Kahl.

become muddy. Constant dampness often is the undoing of water snakes, frequently causing illness in the terrarium. A strip of coarse gravel at the edge of the water section catches the water drops when the animals leave the water. Rocks, root stocks, and branches for climbing, basking upon, and gliding along make up the furnishings of the land section. Water snakes like hiding places, but these should always be easily

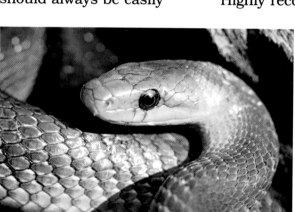

The European Aesculapian Snake, Elaphe longissima, *is very similar to the American rat snakes both in structure and keepability. Photo courtesy Dr. D. Terver, Nancy, France.*

accessible and controllable by the keeper. When in the water, water snakes like to rest on tangles of roots, which also provide them with cover.

The Eurasian Grass Snake or Ringed Snake *(Natrix natrix),* which occurs over much of Europe and northern Asia, is recognized by the conspicuous yellow spots on both sides at the back of the head. It is very shy at first, but the elegant

animals soon become acclimated. Their diet consists chiefly of frogs, but fishes are also taken, although not as readily.

The Dice Snake *(Natrix tessellata),* whose brownish or yellow-brown back exhibits a darker, roughly checkered pattern, is also suitable for keeping in the terrarium. It likes water even more than does the Grass Snake and prefers fishes to amphibians.

Highly recommended is the Viperine Water Snake *(Natrix maura).* The spotting on the brownish or occasionally olive back along with a dark zig-zag band recalls the pattern often present in vipers. The dark-bordered whitish ocelli on the flanks are conspicuous. This species likes to wait in ambush for fishes under water among tangles of roots.

The Common Garter Snake *(Thamnophis sirtalis)* from the United States has many subspecies and very similar related species. It is frequently offered and is bred in captivity. The

animals exhibit a great deal of individual variation and are found in a variety of habitats. They prefer a certain amount of moisture and feed on frogs, insects, and earthworms, but in captivity they sometimes take strips of fish. Garter snakes like to rest on low bushes or on elevated places to sun. When the slender head with the brown-bordered eyes and the darting red tongue pokes out from cover on the slender, striped neck, this is a picture of the utmost elegance and suppleness. Markings and colors are harmoniously in tune with each other, no element too obtrusive. Because of the eye ring this snake's eye loses its staring quality. The tongue, red with black points and deeply forked, darts continually. One is truly captivated by this sight, which has the power to excite the imagination.

Leimadophis poecilogyra is widely distributed in South America and is a beautiful snake. Greenish or red transverse bands are usually present, but the species is extremely variable in coloration. As South Americans, they need warmth. This tropical snake, approximately 70 centimeters long, feels comfortable at a temperature of 23 to 28°C (73 to 82°F). It prefers frogs but eats fishes and occasionally crustaceans. The land section of the aqua-terrarium should be composed of bricks of peat and patches of moss. The peat must not be allowed to become too wet, and the moss must be changed regularly. The fact that these handsome snakes do quite well in the terrarium is a further good quality. Of course, good ventilation of the cage must be provided.

Of the distinctly terrestrial snakes that can get by with a fairly small water container for an occasional bath, the European Smooth Snake *(Coronella austriaca)* is worthy of note. Its prey, which consists of lizards, is strangled before being swallowed. It is not to everyone's taste to watch this, especially since many reptile fanciers, after all, have a close association with lizards. This brownish gray snake has a zig-zag band of spots on the back and is therefore often confused with the vipers.

The Aesculapian Snake *(Elaphe longissima)* of Europe attracts attention because of the elegance of

Dice Snakes, Natrix tessellata. Photo by H. Hansen.

its movements as well as because of its size. It is an excellent climber and is capable of climbing up the narrowest crack in the manner of a chimney sweep. If it ever happens to actually escape from the terrarium, you should first look for it on top of cabinets and bookshelves. In the terrarium it should be provided with good provisions for climbing. This smooth, uniformly brown to olive southern European feeds principally on mice but will not pass up young birds and lizards. Because of its size (up to 1.8 meters) and climbing habits it requires a correspondingly roomy cage.

One of the most beautiful snakes of all is the southern European Leopard Snake *(Elaphe situla)*, which reaches a length of barely 1 meter. On a light brown background are found pairs of bright red to yellow-red, black-edged spots. The spots often flow together into short transverse bands. There is also a striped form. This colorful snake likes dryness and warmth (the bathing dish is visited only prior to molting) and is considered to be somewhat delicate. Apparently, it generally lacks a supply of fresh air in captivity. All snakes are very sensitive to stale air and excessive heat. An over-wintering period of about three months is beneficial for the Leopard Snake. It

Common Garter Snakes, Thamnophis sirtalis, occur in a bewildering variety of similar subspecies and color variants. There also are several other almost identical species of garter snakes in North America. Photo by W. B. Allen, Jr.

must be well nourished. It feeds chiefly on mice.

Young Boa Constrictors (Boa constrictor) seem almost to have been created expressly for keeping in the terrarium. In general, these very quiet animals lie for hours at a time, even all day long, tightly coiled in their favorite spot. They need warmth and a sufficiently large warm water section. The water heater must be installed in a gutter tile to prevent breakage. Make sure that they do not get tangled in the heater cord. A section of the cover of the cage should consist of wire mesh so that the heat

lamp can be installed on top of it.

These snakes feed on mice, rats, and guinea pigs. The killing of the prey animal by constriction takes place quickly as long as the snake has room to strike and apply the coils. It is therefore advisable under certain circumstances to remove the thick climbing branches before feeding. If you hold the food animal in front of the boa with long forcep in such a way that it can get hold of the animal's head or snout on the first strike, then you will accelerate the process of constriction and swallowing. This is important, because sometimes the snake searches for the pointed head of the sacrifice for an interminable time instead of swallowing the animal immediately as usual. If two boas in the same cage fumble around with the food at the same time, they sometimes mix up the prey animals, a mistake

will usually allow themselves to be taken from their cages for feeding. An old blanket is laid on a table and in the middle is placed a fairly large branch on which the snakes like to anchor themselves. From this position they then strike at the unsuspecting food animal.

During and after feeding

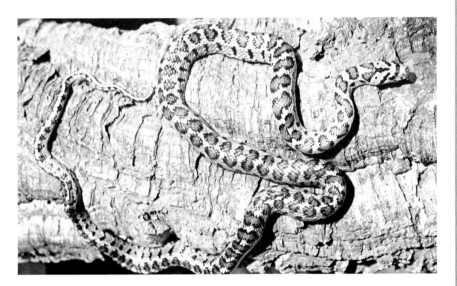

The Leopard Snake of Eurasia, Elaphe situla, *is perhaps the most attractive snake in the area and it is highly prized by hobbyists. Many specimens are superficially similar to the American Corn Snake,* Elaphe guttata. *Photo by K. Knaack.*

that can sometimes have very bad consequences. If in such a case they seize one and the same prey animal at the same time, they usually do not let go; to the contrary, one will also swallow the head of the other along with the prey animal. Usually both snakes die in this upsetting incident. Avoid feeding two or more boas at the same time in one cage. If you have the animals' confidence, they

the snakes understandably are in a state of great excitement. Leave them alone during this procedure. Bring them back to the terrarium with very quiet, slow movements. The safest way is to approach with one hand from below. You should never approach a boa with extended fingers. Sometimes they can be removed from the climbing branch only with difficulty. Gentle, steady pressure on

the tail end helps, and the snake will slowly glide onto the arm of the keeper.

The rearing of young Boa Constrictors is interesting, and you will truly derive great pleasure from these attractive, quiet animals. Juvenile Boa Constrictors are frequently offered. The dark-brown spotted and banded markings on the light brown to tan background merge into a beautiful red-brown color, particularly toward the tail. The flat, clearly set off head has impressive banded markings behind the eyes, which lends the head a somewhat magical appearance.

THE COMPLETELY ILLUSTRATED ATLAS OF REPTILES AND AMPHIBIANS FOR THE TERRARIUM
By Fritz Jürgen Obst, Dr. Klaus Richter, Dr. Udo Jacob
ISBN 0-86622-958-2
TFH H-1102
Audience: Here is a truly comprehensive and beautiful volume covering all the reptiles and amphibians kept in terrariums plus virtually all the oddballs and rarities any hobbyist (or scientist, for that matter) is likely to ever see or want to know about. Illustrated in full color are hundreds of common and rare reptiles and amphibians, invertebrates, food animals, terrarium plants, environments, and diseases, with hundreds more black and white photos and line drawings. But don't think that this book is just pictures—the authoritative and useful text covers thousands of species, the majority of genera, and hundreds of topics dealing with terrarium care and natural history. The alphabetical arrangement makes it easy to find information on almost any topic you can think of, and you can be sure the information is correct and up-to-date.

This volume is the perfect answer to the terrarium keeper's dilemma of attempting to find where an animal originated and what type of habitat it requires. It is the obvious first place to look for a solution or a hint to all your questions while having fun looking at the marvelous photos at the same time.
Hard cover, 8¼" x 12¼", 830 pages
Contains 1,567 full-color photos, 381 drawings, and 168 black and white photos.

REPTILE CARE: An Atlas of Diseases and Treatments
By Dr. Fredric L. Frye
ISBN 0-86622-215-6 (set of both volumes) **TS-165**
This two-volume set has it all. Two beautiful big (10 x 14") and immensely colorful volumes encompass the entire spectrum of reptile maintenance and health care. Feeding, captive husbandry, reproduction in reptiles, plus information about the recognition and treatment of every health-related condition imaginable are only some of the subjects covered in this enormously informative work.
Hard cover, 10 x 14", over 650 pages
Contains more than 1800 full-color photos.

GIANT LIZARDS
By Robert Sprackland
ISBN 0-86622-634-6 **TFH TS-145**
Contents: Introduction; Husbandry; Family Varanidae; Family Helodermatidea; Family Teiidae; Family Agamidae; Family Scincidae; Family Iguanidae; Miscellaneous Giants; Veterinary Care; The Law and Herpetoculture; Careers in Herpetology; Glossary; Bibliography.
Audience: This detailed and up-to-date discussion of the monitor lizards, tegus, large iguanas, and other lizards over about three feet in length stresses captive care and identification. Heavily illustrated in color, it is the only modern discussion of this popular, even if artificial, group of lizards that capture the fancy of so many hobbyists.
Hard cover. Completely illustrated with full-color photos.

SALAMANDERS AND NEWTS:
A Complete Introduction
By Byron Bjorn
Softcover **CO-043S**
ISBN 0-86622-389-4
Audience: This basic book for beginners guides you through the mysterious world of salamanders and newts. It provides all of the information that is necessary for the proper feeding, breeding, and health care, of these popular and highly interesting animals.
Contains over 75 full-color photos and drawings.

PYTHONS AND BOAS
By Peter J. Stafford
ISBN 0-86622-084-4
TFH PS-846
Contents: Natural History;
Pythoninae-True Pythons;
Calabariinae and Loxoceminae-
Burrowing Pythons; Boinae-True
Boas; Erycinae-Ground Boas;
Tropidophiinae and Bolyeriinae
Dwarf Boas; Captive Breeding, The
Care of Boids in Captivity, Informal
Key to the Boid Genera, A Checklist
of Pythons and Boas.
Audience: This is the one book
needed by snake fanciers to
familiarize themselves with this
impressive reptile group. Here's the
first authoritative work on the boas
and pythons, an attractive—and very
colorful—volume that will answer
every question about snake care
and present current information on
boas and pythons in a
comprehensive book.
Hardcover, 198 pages, 5½ x 8"
Contains 110 full-color photos, 22
black and white photos and 60
illustrations.

ATLAS OF SNAKES
By John Coborn
ISBN 0-86622-749-0
TFH TS-128
Contents: Snakes and Man. Snake
Evolution, Classification and
General Biology. Housing for
Captive Snakes. General
Husbandry. Reproduction and
Propagation. Infraorder Scolephidia.
Snake Venoms, Antivenoms and
Treatment of Snakebites. Glossary.
Audience: Intermediate to
Advanced. A survey of the full
variety of snakes. Features a brief
discussion of each genus, arranged
by family and subfamily.
Hardcover: over 400 pages,
completely illustrated.

KINGSNAKES AND MILK SNAKES
By Robert Markel
ISBN 0-86622-664-8
TFH TS-125

Contents: Introducing kingsnakes;
Kingsnakes in captivity; Albinism;
Diseases and Parasites;
Recognition of the kingsnakes; Gray
Banded Kingsnake; Prairie
Kingsnake; Common Kingsnake;
San Luis Potosi Kingsnake; Sonoran
Mountain Kingsnake; Ruthven's
Kingsnake; Milk Snake; Mountain
Kingsnake; References; Glossary.

Audience: A comprehensive
coverage of all the species and
subspecies of kingsnakes and milk
snakes, genus *Lampropeltis*. All four
dozen taxa (and many variants) are
described in detail and illustrated in
full color by specially-drawn color
diagrams. Nearly all the subspecies
are also illustrated in color
photographs. Special sections on
husbandry cover breeding and
feeding problems. Maps. High
school and above.
Hardcover, 6 x 9", 160 pages
Over 150 full-color photos and
drawings

ENCYCLOPEDIA OF TURTLES
By Dr. Peter C. H. Pritchard
ISBN 0-87666-918-6
TFH H-1011
Contents: Turtle Identification.
Turtle Structure and Function. Turtle
Evolution and Fossil History. Emydid
Turtles. Land Tortoises. Mud, Musk,
and Snapping Turtles. Soft-Shelled
Turtles. Monotypic Turtle Families.
Sea Turtles. Side-Neck Turtles.
Turtle Conservation and Exploration.
Turtles in Captivity. Two
Appendices. Glossary.

Audience: This book is of value to
pet keepers, scientific turtle experts,
and everyone in between, being
particularly mindful of the intelligent
general naturalist and the academic
zoologist who has use for an
overview of the turtles within the
covers of a single volume.
Hardcover, 5½ x 8½", 896 pages
358 color photos, 304 black and
white photos, 70 line drawings

CUSTOMARY U.S. MEASURES AND EQUIVALENTS	METRIC MEASURES AND EQUIVALENTS

LENGTH

1 inch (in)		= 2.54 cm
1 foot (ft)	= 12 in	= .3048 m
1 yard (yd)	= 3 ft	= .9144 m
1 mile (mi)	= 1760 yd	= 1.6093 km
1 nautical mile = 1.152 mi		= 1.853 km

1 millimeter (mm)		= .0394 in
1 centimeter (cm)	= 10 mm	= .3937 in
1 meter (m)	= 1000 mm	= 1.0936 yd
1 kilometer (km)	= 1000 m	= .6214 mi

AREA

1 square inch (in^2) = 6.4516 cm^2
1 square foot (ft^2) = 144 in^2 = .093 m^2
1 square yard (yd^2) = 9 ft^2 = .8361 m^2
1 acre = 4840 yd^2 = 4046.86 m^2
1 square mile(mi^2) = 640 acre   = 2.59 km^2

1 sq centimeter (cm^2) = 100 mm^2 = .155 in^2
1 sq meter (m^2)   = 10,000 cm^2 = 1.196 yd^2
1 hectare (ha)   = 10,000 m^2 = 2.4711 acres
1 sq kilometer (km^2) = 100 ha   = .3861 mi^2

WEIGHT

1 ounce (oz)	= 437.5 grains	= 28.35 g
1 pound (lb)	= 16 oz	= .4536 kg
1 short ton	= 2000 lb	= .9072 t
1 long ton	= 2240 lb	= 1.0161 t

1 milligram (mg)		= .0154 grain
1 gram (g)	= 1000 mg	= .0353 oz
1 kilogram (kg)	= 1000 g	= 2.2046 lb
1 tonne (t)	= 1000 kg	= 1.1023 short tons
1 tonne		= .9842 long ton

VOLUME

1 cubic inch (in^3)		= 16.387 cm^3
1 cubic foot (ft^3)	= 1728 in^3	= .028 m^3
1 cubic yard (yd^3)	= 27 ft^3	= .7646 m^3
1 fluid ounce (fl oz)		= 2.957 cl
1 liquid pint (pt)	= 16 fl oz	= .4732 l
1 liquid quart (qt)	= 2 pt	= .946 l
1 gallon (gal)	= 4 qt	= 3.7853 l
1 dry pint		= .5506 l
1 bushel (bu)	= 64 dry pt	= 35.2381 l

1 cubic centimeter (cm^3)   = .061 in^3
1 cubic decimeter (dm^3) = 1000 cm^3 = .353 ft^3
1 cubic meter (m^3)   = 1000 dm^3 = 1.3079 yd^3
1 liter (l)   = 1 dm^3 = .2642 gal
1 hectoliter (hl)   = 100 l   = 2.8378 bu

TEMPERATURE

CELSIUS° = 5/9 (F° − 32°)   FAHRENHEIT° = 9/5 C° + 32°

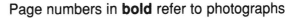

Page numbers in **bold** refer to photographs